I0192485

LICHTWELTVERLAG
VIENNA, AUSTRIA

JAHN J KASSL

THE BIOGRAPHY OF JESUS

MY LIFE ON EARTH

PART ONE

1st English Print Edition 2016

Copyright © 2006 by Lichtwelt Verlag, Vienna, Austria
Lichtweltverlag JJK OG, Albertgasse 49/13+14, A-1080 Vienna, Austria
E-mail: office@lichtweltverlag.com
Telephone: +43 (1) 944 65 09
Telefax: +43 (1) 253 30 33 1750

www.lichtweltverlag.com

Translation from the German original by Rüdiger Franz Rauskolb
Cover photo, book design and author photo © 2015 Jens Schnabel, Munich
Printed by CreateSpace, An Amazon.com Company, for details see the last page

ISBN 978-3-9503509-3-7

"In order to attain your Divinity,

it is necessary to fully accept your Humanity."

Given from JESUS CHRIST

CONTENT

EXPLANATION

"JESUS CHRIST and the consciousness of SANANDA are ONE!
Therefore it is the ONE consciousness that takes effect through this
book."

At the beginning, I would like to mention, and I thank my editor, that
she pointed this out to me, so that the differently signed chapters by
HIM (by JESUS or SANANDA) do not confuse you.
It is always HE who talks to us, and his eternal name, his vibrational
name, is SANANDA.

Every human Being carries such an eternal name, but is in most
cases unknown to us. We bring our multidimensional reality to the
surface through this name, and therefore our true Being is apparent
to all in the universe. The personal signature, whereby we express
our entire potential!

JESUS OF NAZARETH, the JESUS, who is familiar to us and for
2000 years played such a significant role in the history of mankind,
therefore is the incarnation of SANANDA, the blissfully unconditional
Love from eternity.

The Christ Consciousness has been anchored on earth through JESUS
(therefore JESUS CHRIST), in order to enable for every human Being
access to his I AM presence. Both expressions (Christ Consciousness
and the I AM) describe the unconditional Love that for us here on
earth is called for to realize. Therefore HE has come and due to his
life as a human Being among humans, the all-penetrating power of
love is accessible to all human Beings since then, so that we, each
one of us, awaken into our divinity.

Into the Christ Consciousness and into our I AM presence.

That was the meaning of JESUS'S life and work on earth, and through the omnipresent consciousness of SANANDA, this assignment has been fulfilled. This book describes HIS life in Jerusalem, therefore he signs quite often with JESUS CHRIST, also so that we may easily recognize HIM, because his name is very familiar to us. Where the facts of the told story are less important, the comprehensive consciousness of SANANDA comes forward, and therefore those chapters are signed accordingly.

In summary, we experience in this biography JESUS and his omnipresent loving consciousness that is expressed in the name of SANANDA. I interpret this as a small "task" for us so that we may also gradually release our fixed opinions of JESUS OF NAZARETH in that respect. So that we direct our attention to the "carrier essence", the essence, whereby Jesus was who he is.
Since Eternity, from Eternity and in Eternity.

JESUS CHRIST or SANANDA?
It is always ONE power that touches you, the ONE who accompanies you, the ONE consciousness that loves you immensely.

The journey through JESUS'S life is exciting and for some human Being may also be shocking, because the actual events strongly deviate from the story we were told so far. More than ever the innocence of humanity will be the theme in the final part. But everyone who starts on this path will be richly gifted — *with the knowledge that liberates us and lifts all guilt from our shoulders.*

A truly exciting journey is again ahead of you.

In Love
Jahn J Kassl

INTRODUCTION

It was a time of great changes.
Human suffering, misery, despair and the lack of any consciousness about the true issues of life were widely distributed. Wars, violence and daily rudeness were realities, and a life free of it was inconceivable.

I was born into this time in order to anchor a totally new energy on earth — *the Love.*

In order to bring new vistas of things into the rigid structures and to human Beings separated from Oneness. And even though religions, confessions and divine worship were ordinary, there was a lack of inner ability to raise one's consciousness and to look beyond one's limitations.

My birth has been prophesied.
A lot has been written, much has been assumed, and yet much is not correct and has been authored according to conditions then prevailing.

I am JESUS CHRIST, and my message is then as today:

Love one another, become capable of loving unconditionally in order to go into God's arms.

This is the path of the King and you find fulfillment only in it.
Do justice to your destiny and live the universal realization of Love.
I have come and have lived among human Beings and with human Beings in order to bring this energy unto earth.

Much is not known and is not reported as it really happened and is. Therefore, these transmissions shall adjust, bring new perspectives about the events and enable a new understanding.

The Earth is in transformation. And the time is ripe to bring clarity and truth to the events of my life on earth. All deceptions fall off, and the Light brings everything out into the open what often over a very long time has waited for the return.

I am amongst you, and the salvation of mankind and earth happen — NOW.

I am amongst you and in your heart, as you recognize, as you open yourself to this truth. Not in a faraway time and not in the Beyond!

The healing of Planet Earth is in full force and my reappearance an existing fact.

Blessed are those who recognize me.
Blessed are those who see me.

Blessed are those who have an open heart.
Blessed are those who welcome me.

Blessed are those who enter into eternal Life.
Blessed are those who submit to this process of transformation.

Blessed are those who awaken.
Blessed are those who unveil their true essence to look into God's almightiness and to recognize their own divinity.

Blessed are those who go forth and love
who are where there is darkness still,
and who bring light to those who are still afraid of it.

Blessed are those who carry joy inside,
who peacefully leave traces behind in God's Oneness.
For the benefit of mankind and for the recovery of Mother Earth.

Therefore, wake up, beloved child of humanity, and recognize that the time of my reappearance has come.

Be ready to receive me as I come.
Hear my knocks and open your door.
So that I may enter your home, and so that you may ascend in purity and in full consciousness of your power, and so that you ignite your light according to your true destiny.

Praise to the one who comes.
I am amongst you.
Now and in Eternity.

PROLOGUE

I have come to sow peace, joy and Love.
But what have you made out of it?

Instead of peace there are wars, instead of joy there is suffering and
instead of Love there is Hate. You were deceived generation for
generation and you were kept far from my true message. Suffering was
lifted to a great necessity so that human Beings believed that suffering
is the only way to attain holiness. My death on the cross was put in
front of your eyes as an example, and your spirituality was supposed
to find reflection in this suffering.

You were deceived, beloved Mankind.
Thoroughly and knowingly cheated.

My death on the cross never happened!

This information is very important so that you stop to identify
yourselves with this suffering. Suffering does not lead to salvation
that so many of you strive for.

Beloved children of Mankind, I neither died on the cross nor have I
been crucified. The scriptures of Peter bear witness of what has been
withheld from you. It is a great error in your history, and those who
are responsible for it have loaded a great burden on themselves. As
a result of this erroneous description of my life and my death, an
infinite amount of suffering came to earth. Suffering was supposed
to ennoble you and be noble. But it is destructive and causing so
much pain, but the whole earth has been covered by it.

Wars were waged in the name of suffering and in the name of the Cross; all joy was taken from you. The possibility of peace was withheld from you, and hate has been and still is a reality on earth.

How many wars, how much destruction of life on earth and how much personal suffering were in your daily life!
This happens because you believed in the wrong image of my message for hundreds of years.

Also you were robbed of the joy in the beauty of sexuality and the freedom to live it out of the heart. It was declared to you that this is something indecent, something animalistic. You were and you are still asked to kill the sexuality in you. And again you shall force yourself, and again suffering is created where there should be joy.

The church is a man-made institution. It has not been my will to create a society that holds human Beings in suffering, lack of joy and fear. The historical events are known, and the foundation of the Roman Catholic Church carries the stamp of human Beings, and not my seals.

The so-called key transfer to Peter has never happened!

Also the description that I was never married is false!

Many of my companions at that time were women. Besides my mother MARY, my wife MARY MAGDALENE and women, who were close to my disciples. It was a mixed community.

For a man at that time and in this religious, cultural reality it was fully customary and nearly required to get married. We were meant for each other, and in this life on earth our love fully blossomed. MIRIAM FROM BETHANY was not a whore and not a sinner, as people like to portray her. She was and is a high initiate of Life, and at that time we were intimately joined together.

The wedding at Cana was our wedding.
I was her bridegroom and she was my bride.

How important this information is, and how much it has been
missing until now from earth and foremost from human Beings with
a strong catholic background. The most natural form of relationship
on earth, the one between a man and a woman, has been made
maggoty for you, and you were kept far away from the joy of such a
relationship. Without this joy you could not blossom, and therefore
you were cheated out of it.

I tell you this so that you know and now it is time that all lies come
out into the light. Also the untruths, the false portrayals and conscious
lies about my life on earth two thousand years ago. There is so much
that needs clarification and a new consideration, and this transmission
will dissolve old pictures of mine and will bring a new consciousness.

Finally the freedom that many human Beings yearned for, the peace,
the joy and love. And it was always the Love that accompanied me.
My heart had so much of it, and everywhere it exuded. Just by itself.

Many "miracles" simply happened, when human Beings saw me.
The Light that emanated from me healed all and everyone, as the
personal development allowed for it.

I travelled a lot, and we went from location to location. For my
companions, the disciples, the days were always exciting and full
of surprises. I myself was open, and like a channel the Light of the
Father flowed through me.

It was my assignment to bring Light and Love, and to anchor these
energy qualities in the earth. But the time and the events in Jerusalem
came to a crisis, and so the day came when I left Jerusalem.

The last Supper points to that fact.
It was a festivity of departure, and all were gathered. We ate dates and figs and shared the bread. It was my farewell from my friends and life companions. Also from my wife and my mother. There were not just twelve at this festivity, but substantially more, and all came to say goodbye. The history let you believe that after that my crucifixion happened.

All these descriptions are untrue and false!

Still before I began to work publicly, something happened that touched me profoundly and most painfully: the decapitation of my beloved JOHN THE BAPTIST. I loved him so much, and it happened very quickly. It was clear to me that my ministry in this area would be of limited duration. And it is true, it took about three years before I said goodbye and over many paths came to India, at the border to Nepal.

My message was full of Love and joy. Full of gusto and of deep divine inspiration. And many have understood these, but many did not partake in these insights. Until today.

Now mankind receives the opportunity to attain new information about the past events. So that you may accept, what I had given you already then.

Begin with your own discovery and find joy and love.

This message is unchanged, and due to these facts you can easier liberate yourself from the old energies causing so much suffering. There is so much more that is withheld from you, but now let's call it an end. The whole truth is now given to you. The truth regarding the events how they have actually happened, and not what was conveyed to you so far.

In the next chapters you will experience much about my words and my deeds and how they should be understood.

God is with you.

BIRTH AND CHILDHOOD

Beloved Brothers and Sisters of the Light.

My heart is filled with joy that so much energy of love is in you. And this inner light shines ever more so that it visibly for us flows into the whole Universe.

Today I give you a view into the time of my birth, my childhood and the experience of life of my early years, in the life of Jesus on earth.

My birth had been prophesied and therefore my mother Mary knew out of which power the fruit in her belly grew from. And the stars pointed the way for the Wise Men to us in order to deliver their gifts of praise. This happened in the spring of the 4th year of your calendar.

My childhood went off without worrying and I breathed the healthy as well as loving environment of my parents. Even that we travelled frequently I always had the feeling of absolute safety and within me the trust in all that IS, was strengthened. So I grew up, my brothers were born and my sisters.

My first years were shaped in the feeling of love and the "having arrived" on earth.

My parents were fully conscious of their assignment and everywhere where it seemed necessary to them and when it was possible they accompanied me in a wonderful manner. Slowly I was made aware of my assignments. Much was preordained by tradition, as I was from the house of David and this fact explains that I should adopt the title of a king. But until then there was still some time.

We write the year 12.

At that time our family was in Egypt, in Alexandria. My father worked in the profession of a "carpenter". But this description does not fully correspond to it, because the whole planning, from the drawings to the construction of the house, were to be done. At that time I was introduced into the Jewish community of Alexandria, and it was a very beautiful time of learning and understanding.

I spent entire days in the rooms of the temple reading the scriptures. We lived in a small house and our family lacked nothing. Everything was always there that cared for the physical wellbeing as well as our spiritual growth.

It was a feeling of absolute trust in God that accompanied our family, wherever we were. And my parents had this deep inner realization so that they never worried.

Slowly the temple became my home. I spent more and more time there, and the brothers of this community were open and I was able to spread out my questions to them. My inner need to learn and to gain the knowledge about the last things grew.

In this time I also began to accept the contact with my teachers within me. Due to my intuition and the capacity to hear "God's voice", it was already very early possible for me to attain an understanding that baffled many human Beings. The interpretation of the scriptures was a fundamental issue of so many discussions with the scribes. In Alexandria I was able to practice this and gradually I attained a comprehensive knowledge about our assignments and our life on earth.

As the situation in Jerusalem quieted down and it seemed to be of permanence, we returned and when I was at the age of 12 I was officially introduced into the local temple.

My acquired knowledge about the scriptures and my way of presenting it, surprised many and some were in awe because of it.

Jerusalem's Jewish community was dedicated to the scriptures word by word and the easiness with which I talked about it as well as my interpretations were not really desired.

While my family grew, after JACOB followed SIMON, then came JUDAS, my path began to spread out in front of me.

Often I forgot the "time" around me while I listened to God's answers. The power of Love began to expand within me and often it seemed that I merged with the whole world.

"The freedom which I bring is not of this world, and yet it will save this world."

I grew into this consciousness.

My daily life was the one of a youth in that area. To help my father in his work, whereby to learn his skills, the play with the siblings, whereby we had a great ball game, similar to your soccer, and often we were many young human Beings who shared the joy in it. Among them were later companions along the way, and in this time my capacity for healing also became apparent.

Wherever somebody injured himself I tried to give my healing power. Either I put my hands on the painful section of the afflicted one, or I concentrated and sent "light bundles" into the energy field of human Beings.

This capacity attained years later a great strength, and wherever I was, a light-force emanated from me that changed human Beings and healed them. And in these early years I tested this divine blessing.

In those years my mother was busy to provide for the family, and her softness and love towards all human Beings was for me a source of pure insight that showed itself through her actions in daily life. For her there was never good or evil and any judgment was alien to her. So she never talked bad about somebody else and her heart was full of kindness and mindfulness.

A deep inner understanding for the partner carried the love of my parents, and often I had the impression that this love grew over the years, because I could see it in their eyes how close their hearts were in reality.

I was able to unfold in this environment, and the preparations for my mission found their continuation in the year 18, whereby I began to absorb the "pure teachings".

My acceptance in the Essene congregation outside of Jerusalem built the "logical" continuation of my path in education and growth. Understanding and becoming.

In those years I attained the essential capacities and all the knowledge about the true reason for the existence of us human Beings here on earth. My brothers in Qumran transmitted much to me, yet I had received the essential part through my ever-expanding light channels.

My heart was unconditionally open and so I was able to join in fulfillment with the world beyond ours. These were the years toward becoming adult in physical as well and foremost in spiritual manner.

In this time we met frequently, because JOHN was also a brother in the congregation, somewhat older and on his way to spread the message of purity, rightfulness, humbleness, clarity and dedication to God — far advanced.

Already as children we recognized each other, and even though we did not see each other often, a common quietly felt familiarity and an understanding surrounded us, beyond words.

What joined us was the dedication to God and the knowledge about our assignments. And in those years the recognition strengthened about the significance of our birth in that part of the earth. Often we sat for hours on a rock or in the shadow of a tree, in the sand of the desert or in the courtyard of the temple.

We talked about our Father in Heaven and how the eternal return into the Oneness may be attained. Yet most of the time we spent in silence. In rapt contemplation and joined with the Source that brought us here, brought us together and enlightened us.

Finally the time had come and JOHN went there in order to unfold his assignment all by himself. There was a great farewell festivity and many tears were shed, foremost tears of joy. Because a goodbye is never forever and everybody knew that the mystery shall be fulfilled. And everybody felt a deep connection to his brothers, beyond all limitations that our body puts on us.

The following years made him widely known, because his sharp mind and his ruthless dedication to the truth did not remain unnoticed.

Meanwhile I went through my "processes", my consciousness increased steadily, it grew what was assigned to me and I unfolded my divine consciousness.

Full of peace I said goodbye to my brothers in order to begin my for the moment "last" journey.

I took off for Egypt, Syria and to Greece. Yet this journey guided me into my heart, into my inner and I faced my eternal expression of Love in the consciousness of All-That-Is of all Life.

While this happened I visited many villages and cities. Thereby I studied human Beings and their behavior, their intentions and motivations.

Their story was an open book in front of me, I read their thoughts and could see their feelings. It sharpened my sight and the answers about the significance of a human life were given to me.

Over and over again I went into retreat and often I was immersed for days in conversation with my Father in Heaven. With the heavenly messengers, the Masters beyond the veil and with the brothers and sisters of my spiritual home.

In these years of travel I finally turned toward my all-encompassing Being and I fully accepted what was given to me. So I grew into the shoes that were fitted to me, now my family were human Beings of the whole earth, all living creatures and every consciousness in God's Creation.

When I returned to Jerusalem, I was a different one and yet I was who I always have been: WHO I AM.

"....and so I stepped into JOHN'S water and my heart was filled with joy, the sandals were left behind on the shore and when the water of the river Jordan washed around me, a great peace spread, all around us and in the hearts of human Beings. So it was sealed what had been destined from Eternity. The omnipresent union of human Beings with God, the union of Heaven and Earth."

Beloved Children of God,
We are all one and joined by the power of omnipresent Love.

Accept this fact and unfold your beauty.
The oneness can only be experienced.
And truly, we ALL are one.

You are infinitely loved.

JESUS CHRIST

THE BREAD OF LIFE

Beloved Children of Mankind,
It is time to bring you into the knowledge of what happened then
and the truth will set you free. Your hearts will blossom and the wait
for salvation will be fulfilled.

I am the one whom you know as JESUS CHRIST.
And today I give you these messages through this human Being, who
is very familiar to me; and who since time eternal has been joined
with me. Trust this biography, because this channel is pure and clear.

Therefore let us turn to today's topic and again it is the all-
encompassing, unconditional Love that you shall experience.
For all, who are of good will, for those, who long for it and search
for their hidden truth.

When I dwelled among you in a human body, questions about love
were a daily occurrence and many human Beings could not find the
possibility to develop their capacity for love and let it become real.
Too great was the power of outer circumstances. Because in a world
of lovelessness it was difficult to live the love.

And today I also hear your questions.
How shall I love? How can I succeed when social coldness, societal
hardship and intolerance are a daily occurrence? Where should I
begin, without thereby coming to harm myself?
I hear these questions and they are the same, for thousands of years,
since the downfall of Atlantis. That point in time marked the beginning
of darkness on earth. The fallback into the deep, destructive power of
human ignorance.

After the destruction of Atlantis a totally different humanity developed. It was the last step into total materiality, this physical dimension. God's Light of love could not reach human Beings any more and thousands of years of wars, destruction, the misuse of every kind and the darkness began.

It was such a giant step into the darkness for human Beings that the whole universe felt great respect and love for you.

Will you ever find your way back into the Light?
Will you ever return to your Being of Love?

Over time you were schooled and trained. You were born and after a short life you came back to spirit world. There you received further schooling, in order to progress in the following rebirth and in order to be guided closer toward the secret of your eternity. You were born, died and were reborn. Many times and out of free will.

Now the end of time is here.

The darkness dissolves and the divine Light floods the Earth. Incessantly it expands and for the first time, for a long time, your questions, your begging and your turning toward the Light find a — direct echo. The time of enslavement, the time of hate and the lack of love is gone. This new age leads you again back into your Being. You ask your questions — for the last time.

Therefore, how shall you love?
Initially please accept that love does not know any limitations!
It is always absolute and out of your unconditional behavior you can create this reality.

Therefore love unconditionally. All and everyone.
Make no exceptions.

Your "enemy" shall be your exam, your test. Transform your inner energies into Love. Release yourself from old, hindering emotions. But foremost release yourself from your anxieties.

Today your love falls on fertile ground the fear of disappointment has no justification any longer.

The energy of love is *the* energy for this age.

Whereby the earth renews, ascends and brings God's actions to conclusion, the Light of Love guides you also back to perfection.

The past ages have accumulated tremendous powers of suffering and hate. This force have to discharge themselves and thereby it comes presently to unusually many natural catastrophes, to wars and to spontaneous discharges of fear energy. But do not be afraid, it is necessary and a purifying process that leads to permanent peace.

Please begin to love. And love *yourself* first.
Look at your heart, look inside and observe your feelings.
Where do fears or unresolved conflicts come up in you?

Call on ARCHANGEL MICHAEL or me so that we may lift your burdens. Because your liberated heart is the prerequisite in order to absorb the divine Light of Love. Thereby your fear to live the Love — will be overcome.

You create your own reality.
This commonly valid divine law determines your being-here.

Begin to listen to your feelings. Ask your heart what is good for you. Practice in it, success is certain for you, as you do not despair and patiently understand to celebrate your small improvements.

As soon as you found yourself again in this new reality you will be fully in your divine power. What has hindered you is gone and you love. Now you perceive the world differently. Each suffering has been taken from you and pain is gone forever.

Now it is the time when your self-transformation bears fruit. And you do not have to wait for another life, for another death of your body. You create this new reality. *Now.*

Dare to take this step out of darkness into the Light.
The time for it has finally arrived. Finally and definitely.

After you have taken the first steps into your heart, you will notice immediately that around you changes happen. In this age of the return of Mother Earth and her children into divine union transformations happen in front of your eyes. Be ready for miracles because there will be many of them.

Your love transforms the world.
The social hardship and the deformities in society will disappear as you let go of your "hardship" and your personal "deformities".

You affect so much and now the time is ripe for it in order to finally find salvation. Therefore purify your thoughts, clear up your emotions and be clear in your actions.

Observe yourself and allow yourself to change.
Allow being you again.
Permit yourself to look at your mirror image.
The veil that you have denied yourself so far has become thin.
Push it to the side and look at your divinity.

It is the Love and always it that heals you, redeems you and that brings you peace.

To love, freely and unconditionally, you are destined for it. And therefore you also came this time again to earth. Each human Being on this planet has the until now hidden life assignment:

To love in order to shine your light into Creation.

The time has come for the inclusion of Mother Earth into the expanding Creation, as a jewel vibrating in the divine Light. And the complete healing of all life on earth is at the end of this process.

By redeeming your fears and destructive feelings, patterns and blockages, you perform your part in this transformation. It is *your* very personal contribution. And nobody else can do this for you.

Turn now to your inner world, your soul, in order to take courage so that you lift your sight, stretch out your hands and so you may be able to say:

"I am ready to accept this gift, to love my freedom."

Notice how the world has become another while you read this.
In this instant, do you feel freer, without worry and uplifted?
It is because your heart energy has been activated and your inner strength has been awakened.

You are in your center. There is no fear. No hate can take possession of you. Confidence, courage and love — you experience it now.

So multiply these instances after you have put the book aside.
Be conscious that you can maintain this energy level. It just takes a little bit of practice and your consistency. Out of moments become many moments until you fully immerse yourself in this energy of Love and bail from it. Day for day and at every hour.

This spring never runs dry and your heart contains this ever-filling vessel.

The divine nutrition for Creation.
You are always well fed.

"....the bread fell from the sky like rain and people did not suffer from hunger."

The bread of Life and the eternal spring of living water.

"...and five thousand human Beings were fed from five loafs of bread and two fishes."

God's word chased away the hunger of five thousand. And indeed all were well fed. Fish and bread were not enough and when I began to speak they forgot their hunger. They listened to me and thereby this "miracle" happened. My brothers distributed what they still had, yet all felt well fed.

Over the years this event was falsified and was taken verbatim. Thereby it was a miracle, but not one of the kinds that you are being told. God's word alone satisfies and his Love quenches the thirst. That is the way it was then and so it is also today.

In these parables you find the eternally nourishing bread and the water of Life. The awakened heart incorporates the word instantly and nourishes itself from it. The nutrition for your soul. And is your soul satisfied at first, and then you are not hungry anymore.

You forget your thirst, because you have drunk from the water of Life. You forget your hunger, because you have eaten from God's bread.

God's word has become Light and it settles in your heart.

Now go there and love, until you are fulfilled, and until you have fully nourished yourselves from the God's water and bread.
Go there and bear witness, the time has come for it.

So I say goodbye for today and please always be reminded that I am always with you.

My Love is always with you, all days.

Adonai.
JESUS SANANDA

THE DEATH OF JOHN

JOHN had already been held captive for several weeks. Human Beings had already gotten "used" to it and the protests subsided. His disciples were able to visit him without hindrances, because the guards enabled this by giving them some coins.

JOHN THE BAPTIST was widely known and his speeches fell on fertile ground. The reason for his detention was that the Romans saw in him a man who could cause unrest in the population. Even though JOHN never called for the use of force his messages were so revolutionary that many militant groups felt encouraged to go against Rome.

To be emphasized are the Zealots who did not shy away from a confrontation with Rome. Also for this group JOHN was a prophet, for many even the redeemer, who will liberate the enslaved people from the yoke of the Romans.

For JOHN there was nothing more distant than this.
He preached the turning back, the humility and godly actions. Strongly rooted in pure faith that should bring human Beings closer to GOD.
As a brother from the Essene congregation he had all the tools in order to inhale new life into the Jewish traditions and to assist human Beings to true spirituality.

Long before I began to act, he was active and unfazed by the events around him, he verbalized what others were thinking. Many times he held a mirror in front of the Priests or even in front of the King, and ashamedly they had to accept his strength.

The Priests reluctantly and the King saw in him a "madman", and as long as there was peace and quiet in the population, he let him go on. Yet when this changed, JOHN was arrested. And weeks passed, and then months.

During that time I began to act.
I spoke of God's Kingdom, of Love and human Beings listened to me. There were more and more of them.

I was able to give healings to many and many a miracle happened during that time. Lame ones were able to walk and crippled ones were permanently healed. My reputation spread, while JOHN in his prison cell began to understand.

In comparison to him, I did not interpret the laws verbatim and generally speaking my messages had a wider radius. For me all were equal in Creation and we were joined together through the reality of love. For me the asceticism was not in the foreground, but the abundance as soon as you attained trust in God.

There were differences in our messages, but in its essence they were equal: *The dedication to God, our Father in Heaven.*

We were very close and in the Essene congregation I was able to experience and learn much through him. The clarity and his courage were unsurpassed.

His disciples reported to him in prison almost daily what was happening on the outside and what turns my life took. During this time JOHN recognized fully who I was and what the essence of my message was.

"Is he the chosen one?"

This question occupied him until the end and finally he recognized me as the one who I am. He knew it already during the baptism in the river Jordan, but once in a while doubts crept into him, because I however deviated from the strong Jewish religious traditions.

We had our assignments. He was a trailblazer for me and he performed this task in perfection. Like it was already said, he had already been detained for months. One actually expected him to be released soon. But it came to be totally different.

The King came under pressure from Rome, because he could not control the unrests in his territory any longer.

At that time an ambassador from Rome came to visit HEROD. He wanted to be convinced firsthand of Herod's leadership. He was surprised that an "agitator" like JOHN was still alive. Under the threat to present the Emperor a corresponding report that would have meant the loss of power and position for HEROD, in a quick action he decided in the step to have JOHN decapitated.

Yet again the told, and for you familiar story must be corrected, because it was not SALOME, HEROD'S daughter, who had demanded the BAPTIST'S head. No, it was a political decision that HEROD made out of fear for his own wellbeing.

In honor for the guest from Rome a festivity was given. During the festivity, SALOME, HEROD'S daughter, danced. She was very beautiful and an unparalleled sight. HEROD knew this and he wanted to propitiate his guest. But repeatedly the ambassador expressed his disapproval of the situation in Jerusalem. In order to appease his high guest, he gave the order on that same evening to have JOHN killed.

It is also true that HEROD'S wife was not enthusiastic about JOHN, because he had denounced their marriage as "lawless in front of God".

But that was not the reason why events took their course that evening. After all HEROD liked JOHN and quite often he let JOHN come out of his cell in order to have a conversation with him.

The news of JOHN'S decapitation hit human Beings like a lightening rod. The people fell into grief, desperation and anger. I was also deeply hit and it took many conversations with my Father in Heaven, until I retained my divine understanding.

Now it was up to me to go on and to fulfill my mission.
Jerusalem was the place where I should manifest the all-encompassing energy of Love. In constant awareness of my divinity, my assignment began to become reality.

JOHN went into God's arms and he received all honors from the higher realms. His life of that time still has an effect today, in the collective consciousness of human Beings.

Righteousness, Dedication, Being unconditional and the purity of the heart are qualities, which due to his presence arrived in the consciousness of the earth. At a time of deep darkness, in an environment like a powder keg.

He is honored and his heart exudes Love.
And today this Love is also given to you.
Because he is: Among you!

Amen.
JESUS CHRIST

THE POOR IN SPIRIT

"Blessed be the Poor in Spirit because theirs is the Kingdom in Heaven."

There are many human Children who take this statement verbatim, do not know how to interpret the content and thereby do not attain their worth. The self-worth that let you grow, mature, recognize and blossom, into a fully conscious Being of Creation.

Beloved Children of Humanity, let us therefore turn to this statement, so that understanding and a deeper comprehension take a place in your consciousness.

"The Poor in Spirit" are those who have arrived in their heart. They live out of this primal feeling and act among human Beings. Their poverty refers to the fact that they give their mind, only this one is meant here, the space that it should have, but do not allow any expansion beyond that.

The Poor in Mind are those enlightened ones among you, who have found themselves in their all-loving heart. And this happened by allowing their mind, the thinking and experiencing of the world over this part of their Being, foremost to such an extent that it does not create dominance.

The thinking and the mind are a good help for those human Beings in order to get one's bearings here on this earth, but they do not give this authority the all dominating and controlling power. True knowledge and deep love are only born in the heart and this knowledge is familiar to each human Being. Therefore they act out of the heart and their mind performs other functions.

It serves more as a companion, as an authority that knows earthly connections and therefore serves human Beings. The mind has the task to assist you in your decisions and to accompany you. Insights that are born out of the heart have totality and do not need confirmation, because the essential remains hidden to the mind.

To see the truth you can only do well with the heart. Your mind, your thinking keep you grounded and perform the necessary "adaptation measures" as long as you are in your body, so that you do justice to societal rules and their requirements.

Thinking is the greatest hindrance in search of your true essence. If it dominates, you are unable to look behind the curtain. Thereby you would gain the sight for the beyond — and there is the Kingdom in Heaven.

If your thinking and your mind have taken the lead in your life then you cut yourself off from the knowing reality of your heart, the intuition of your inner senses, your feelings and your inner knowledge — the inner voice.

"...the Poor in Spirit."

Here the word "Spirit" has been incorrectly translated. Correctly it should say:

"Blessed be the ones, who lack in thinking, because theirs is the Kingdom in Heaven."

Under no circumstances does it mean the stupid ones or the ones pretending to be stupid. Because stupidity is also another protection not to look inside in order to avoid looking at one's reality. Stupidity is not a quality that fosters the closeness to awareness.

Many human Beings in past centuries have consciously disguised themselves in part and have specifically presented themselves as stupid, because of a verbatim-understood message from the book of books.

Today I give you this message in its initial form and each human Being is invited to think about it and to release the old picture.

A stupid one cannot partake of absolute awareness because he cannot recognize to the necessary extent. Stupidity is always a limitation and many times self-inflicted in order to avoid one's responsibility. It serves like a protective shield that hinders any kind of self-responsibility. Who expects something from a stupid one?

In most cases they can fully live out their "fool's freedom" and thereby they become perpetrators instead of being a victim, because they seduce the environment and fellow men to feelings like pity, impotence, weakness, fear and worry.

But what about those human Beings who are mentally handicapped or were born like that, do they not deserve our sympathy?
Any mental impairment develops due to the karmic potential of an individual. Meaning everything has its cause in the "history" of the human Being. The causes may be different but these incarnations always happen in the consciousness of the development of the individual.

There are no "by chance" in the universe.

Encounter these handicapped human Beings with sympathy. Thereby give them love because it brings healing. These human Beings need open hearts and loving intentions so that their healing may progress. But these human Beings are not meant when I talk about "poverty in thinking".

Meant are those who give thinking and thereby their ego the almightiness and thereby do not grow an inch in their Being. Meant are those who feignedly give themselves as humble, reverent and stupid, hoping to do justice to this section of the bible. It is the false imaginations that repeatedly divert from your true identity. The Kingdom in Heaven has come as soon as you let it into your HEART.

Please do not worry about tomorrow, because everything is there as you are ready to accept it. Remove your thoughts and the mind if you want to enter into your divine essence.

Give the mind the place that it is entitled to. It is a good helper in carrying out daily activities and in "organizing" daily life. But always listen to your inner voice and gradually you will notice that everything comes from the inner that has permanence, and that your thinking often has been a substantial hindrance in order to recognize this.

Your mind, the thinking and your thoughts are connected with your ego. The ego takes form through your thinking and your mind, the form that it needs in order to survive. Therefore the release of your thought patterns immediately affects the dissolution of your ego.

The more you attain your calm and inner silence the stronger the ego will release from you. It can no longer hold on to anything and must go.

This inner transformation will happen in meditation and through dedication to God, from a thinking mind to a feeling heart.

Your awakened consciousness knows, yet your mind guesses sometimes this and sometimes that. Yet you are always aware if you are within yourself.

If you are exclusively present in your mind, then you separate yourself from knowledge and your life does not find fulfillment, a fulfillment that your knowing, feeling and thinking heart can give you.

"...because they inherit the Kingdom in Heaven."

Again it pertains to dissolve the ego and to help the Self to break through. Again it pertains to liberate oneself from hindering thoughts and projections, in order to be clear and to see — what IS.

I have come to guide all human children back into their home in Heaven. And all of us wait that you move in.

"...because the Father in Heaven has many mansions."

Every path is unique and any accompaniment from the spiritual world is appropriate and totally attuned to the individual.

There are many roads to Heaven, yet the last step is the same for all human Beings. It is the step — *into the heart.*
Into knowledge, into understanding, into trust — the absolute *dedication to God.*

It is your feeling heart that awakens as soon as you begin to think with it.

So for today I say goodbye and I bless every one of you.

My Love accompanies you at all time.
JESUS CHRIST

Honored Reader,

The representation of MARY MAGDALENE as a whore and a great
sinner, who in the Light of JESUS turns away from this shameful
doing, follows in the fables of lies of the Catholic Church. The mere
fact that MIRIAM FROM BETHANY simply was JESUS'S wife is
swept under the rug so that the fabricated picture of the Savior and
thereby the dictate of the patriarch can be maintained.

In addition it was necessary for the Roman Catholic Church to
demonize sexuality. As a consequence, sexuality was suppressed and
the natural, free and divine sexual desire in human Beings atrophied,
because it was robbed of its innocence and was loaded with guilt.
Naturally the sexual desire had to find an outlet and it found it in the
over emphasis of it. The sexual disturbances of human Beings and the
"pornographic" world are a clear indication of it.

Thanks to the Roman Catholic Church many human Beings were
inhibited in their capacity for love that expresses itself through sex,
and today on the one hand the over sexualized society is a reality
and on the other hand, the denial of this deep human aspect of love
is still quite common.

In addition the picture of a woman in its totality was permanently
arrested. After EVA in the Old Testament was blamed for the expulsion
from paradise, in the New Testament the misrepresentation of MARY
MAGDALENE strengthens the impression that a woman is the basis of
all-evil; and one cleverly suggests, that sexuality per se is a sin.

And it is the Church in Rome that until today still obstinately and
dismissingly pays homage to this fallacy of their falsified bible,
because until today women at best serve in the church in order to
perform auxiliary functions for the priests.

Yet this "circumcision" of women does not square with the "Anointed Ones" — how should it — and therefore the rampant homosexuality among catholic priests is a, although harmless, peculiarity of it.

In any case truly alarming is the fact of the worldwide prevailing pedophilia in the "Church of Christ". For centuries in heinous regularity revelations become known wherefrom human Beings turn away in horror. This "skeleton in the closet" of the country clerics, the bishops and cardinals, cannot be justified by anything and deserves every attention of an awakened human Being.

Sexuality that is demonized brings forth demonic characteristics and the representations of MARY MAGDALENE abetted this process.

Yet also in the esoteric scene the MARY MAGDALENE fallacy prevails. The "MARY-MAGDALENE-Transfiguration" is responsible for it. The "liberation of women" is being tailored onto her body, as the great goddess in Heaven, as the in all mysteries initiated wife of JESUS.

Increasingly deceptions in awareness take place in the esoteric scene whereby women believe to have been MARY MAGDALENE or at least some soul fragments of JESUS'S wife are established in them. Exactly like more and more men believe to be a reincarnation of JESUS, JOHN THE BAPTIST or one of the disciples, many more women believe to be a reincarnation of MARY MAGDALENE. These developments are a result of the "end time", wherein everything comes out into the open and the fact that the "esoteric" have lost their orientation in themselves a long time ago. For the Catholic Church and for the esoteric scene the simplest and closest explanation is explicitly excluded, namely:

To portray MARY MAGDALENE as a loving wife of JESUS! Nothing more would be necessary.

But both sides have decided to serve up a story that proverbially overstretches any cowhide.

So that human Beings remain dependent and imprisoned in their fears, on the one hand it needs the demonization of the female and on the other hand the unnatural "perversion" of the female picture whereby new fallacies are conjured up and healings must not be forthcoming.

In summary, it is to be stated:

1) The "Fable" of MARY MAGDALENE (Medici-Pope LEO X. (1475-1513) knew: "It is known how much the fable of the CHRIST has served us and ours.") Completes the Church Canon, after the alleged fable of the betrayal by JUDAS and the alleged crucifixion of JESUS. Thereby the Church is sure of its domination over the sexually deprived sheep.

Somebody who experiences sexuality as guilt can rarely experience God's Love, because a human Being is capable for it only then when his energy system has attained a balanced condition and not if he simply blinds out the lower portion of his body and the sexual chakra.

2) Rarely better, nonetheless the lesser evil, is the result of the "MARY-MAGDALENE-Transfiguration" that has been put into the world by the esoteric scene.

The numerous New-Age publications are responsible for the rampant MARY-MAGDALENE-Mania that all women of this time believe to be MARY MAGDALENE.

The common "female", the "sacred sexuality" is being attributed to MARY MAGDALENE in an exaggerated manner since then.

And while this is done human Beings cover up their actual spiritual status, they deny their own suppressed sexual issues and they shy away from working on their perception or they sun themselves in false knowledge.

Who considers himself to be somebody else is neither self nor has he arrived in himself.

Therefore this fallacy can be attributed to two things: Either the lack of self-love, or in the other extreme, the exaggeration of the Ego that impersonates the Self, because the necessary work in perception for self-love has been avoided.

This publication serves so that human Beings may return to themselves through the example of MARY MAGDALENE. It is the command of the hour to let go of "inferiority" and the "spiritual hubris". Thereby there is no need for a MARY MAGDALENE — neither the esoteric one nor the Catholic!

What is needed is solely the unconditional readiness of a human Being to look at what moves his soul and his being into fear:

Freedom, Sexuality and the Light.

"Learn to love yourself."

In Love
JAHN J KASSL

MARY MAGDALENE

"We were meant for each other and in that life our love fully blossomed."

Be greeted beloved earth child,
I am JESUS SANANDA and again I invite you to come on a journey with me.

In the world of the year 27, the year of my marriage with MIRIAM FROM BETHANY. The sister of LAZARUS, a righteous man and with great dedication to the path of pure awareness.

In front of me I see the picture when I visited her the first time. In order to talk to LAZARUS about the marriage. In those days marriages were prearranged, because Jewish tradition required this. According to my ancestry, as the Son from the house of DAVID, as a rightful heir of royal dignity, an appropriate bride was destined for me.
And this was MIRIAM.

A Princess from the house of BENJAMIN and thereby the two most important houses of traditional Jewish history writing were joined in us.

So it was that I saw MIRIAM for the first time in the house of LAZARUS. You would say it was love at first sight. Yet it was recognition, a renewed finding of each other and the knowledge that everything was born out of Eternity.

The marriage was carefully prepared. And when the day came we enjoyed each other in the beauty of our Beings.

Everything was cared for and the mood was wonderfully happy, relaxed and full of joy.

Many times MIRIAM gave me a kiss and at the beginning somewhat shy, her excitement disappeared quickly and our closeness was also sealed physically. During that night she conceived and our first child grew in her body. JOSHUA JOSEF.

The marriage ceremony took place in Cana.
A place outside of Jerusalem and known to you from reports in the bible, as the place, where the miracle of the transformation from water into wine supposedly took place.

Yet here also the truth is simpler than it seems.
Indeed much was drunk and therefore the supply of wine dwindled. I knew that there were barrels in the cellar, which had a deposit of strong wine in them.

As it was the case in many instances, as the wine was not fully finished and this thickened grape juice was by adding water quite delicious. So I asked to fill these barrels with water and the party had again plenty to drink. Many were of the opinion that this wine was even better than the first one that was served. Maybe it was simply the case that the taste buds of the guests were a little strained, therefore they could not recognize the difference anymore. In any case we had enough of this delicious drink and the festivity found its joyous continuation.

Over the years also this story was described differently and in many reports you can read about the "miracle from Cana".
For many writers of that time and foremost the time after, it was very important to picture me as absolutely divine. Thereby my earthly relation of my life gradually disappeared among you.

Many human Beings could not make a connection to their life, to their problems, because I was pictured as infallibly divine and free of any relation to physicality. Therefore one also handed down so many "miracles" and attributed them to me. But, as you see now, everything is much simpler and quite often easy to explain.
Yes, I performed many healings and Jerusalem spoke of them. Yet the miracle from Cana was not one of them and it was a simple process of making wine from water.

In this book you will find additional reports and also corrections, because it is essential that you understand that I was a human Being among human Beings and I had my issues in order to attain the desired salvation.

This closeness is necessary so that you may accept me and thereby enter into your divinity. You will also perform miracles as soon as you have accepted your divinity. Initially this path goes right through your own humanity.

Accept yourself as you are — as a human Being.
Learn to live with yourself and be in peace with yourself.
Learn to love yourself.

That is the Highest of all Laws, because thereby you regain your divinity and enter into the all-encompassing Love of God's power of Creation.

All days I am with you and I do not judge and do not evaluate. Whatever you are preoccupied with and also whenever you are upset or discouraged — I am there.

Accept this fact and allow me to stand by you, to be there for you and use your free will for it. Seize this opportunity and direct your heart toward Heaven, allow yourself this gift.

I am JESUS CHRIST, am constantly concerned about your wellbeing, but your will is honored and without your intent I cannot do much. These are the "rules" on earth that the free will of human Beings is untouchable. We honor these rules, we, who have preceded you to the Father in Heaven.

Your free will dissolves only until you have merged with the Oneness, with the Father in Heaven. Then there is only the absolute knowledge of who you are and your creative consciousness attains its full enfoldment. Then there is no more need for free will, because you are merged with the will of the Father and you act out of this knowledge. It is your will and the will of the Father, which become one intention.

But as long as you are on earth you have this free will. You can decide and manifest your intentions. Therefore decide and accept your responsibility. You have it in your hand and the possibilities for perfection of your existence are infinite. As a human Being bring it into your consciousness that you are infinite. Do not hesitate to dissolve what hinders you in order to be free and in peace.

You know your issues and step into your power by releasing it and thereby enter your eternally loving soul. These are the true miracles, the miracles of transformation of a human Being to his fully conscious divine expression. It does not require "miracles", and no magic, in order to enter into the Kingdom of Heaven.

A miracle is therefore only a miracle because you lack understanding. There is something you cannot explain and you are in awe and you say: "This is a miracle."

When you are awakened, "miracles" will be commonplace, because you are the creator and your actions are divine.

Beloved Children of the Light,

Again I have given you something new in order to make my life understandable among you; in order to take away the shyness to come close to me.

As a human Being among human Beings I spent my days on earth, initially in Jerusalem and later at the border to Nepal. Many travels were given to me; and all what I experienced also served me to my perfection and I grew until I finally entered under the roof of my Father in Heaven.

Much has been given to me and I knew about the developments, and how they will happen. But not everything was clear to me and so I also had to work through in order to understand.

I have come to ignite your inner Light. Not to be regarded as a lifted off Being, as a Being raptured into the distant worlds of the Gods. It was in the interest of the powers on earth to deny you your divinity so that you may be guidable. Yet these times are gone forever!

We all find us again at our starting point in the universe, where there is no separation and everything is experienced out of the Oneness of Being.

The miracles, which I performed, you will also do and even greater ones. So allow me to accompany you and accept what today, now, and by means of this biography, is given to you.

My heart is filled with joy to be able to give you these messages. The Blessing of the Almighty is with you.

So be it.
JESUS SANANDA

TO BE REBORN

"You must be reborn in order to enter the Kingdom of God."

I am JESUS CHRIST and my love is with you wherever you may be.

Let us now turn to this subject.
What does it imply to be reborn and what is meant by it?
To be reborn means to find back to one's reality. The retrieval of your full consciousness, the knowledge about who you really are.

The understanding that everything is an illusion and that your true core of your Being contains all attributes of divinity.

The rebirth is the attainment of your self-consciousness on this level of All-That-Is, on earth. As soon as all deceptions and obstructions have fallen off from you, will you be clear in your perception and you arrive in your intimacy. To be reborn means to return to your origin.

Liberated from the blindness and the shackles of this reality you recognize who you are. This is your rebirth. It is the becoming One with you and with the wellspring of All-That-Is.

This statement does not mean the physical rebirth. The cycle of birth and death, the ever-returning souls in human bodies ends as soon as you awaken in your eternal, single and true Being!

Of this rebirth, of this awakening we are talking about. Of this last step — toward your wholeness.

For many it is difficult to understand how life strings to life until finally the "last" step has been taken so that one must not be born again. All those human Beings who full of longing turn their heart to God know that their stay on earth now finds its end.

Those who cannot understand this "logic" of the Creator or want to, will be given further possibilities in order to liberate themselves from all the deceptions and of the illusion that is contained in the life on earth, so that every one can free himself from the ideas, the thoughts, the emotional patterns and the blockages.

The physical rebirth is necessary in order to mature on the path to realization and to attain the final becoming reborn.

It is the birth into freedom.
Into Joy.
Into Peace.
Into the all-encompassing Love.

Your heart is pure and interlaced with God's Light.
The essence of Creation shines from you.

"...in order to enter the Kingdom of God."

The Kingdom of Heaven is your home.
The "place", where you originated from.
You just forgot it, but now you remember.

You attain the knowledge about your home by releasing irritating feelings and thoughts. The more you release the sooner unfolds this gift in front of you. Thereby you enter under your roof, into the House of the Father and your eternal Mother.

You have arrived and entered your eternal home.

The heavenly realms are so close, because it is in you. If you recognize it the doors open so that you may put down what still hinders you in order to live fully in the consciousness of your nature.

To be reborn is mandatory and only through this transformation into the Light you do arrive in your fulfillment. Thereby your meaning of life, your assignments and your mission fulfill themselves.

You discover your divinity even though the absence of God is being pretended. To live the Love, even though you do not always feel like it and foremost, even though so much horror and hate covers the earth.

It is your task to uncover your eternal core of Being. You attain your beauty and you give this energy back to earth. Beauty creates wellbeing and much ugliness disappears. Your consciousness creates a new reality.

It is your steady being reborn; you liberate yourself from your hate, from fear and from the destructive energies and you thereby affect the awakening of your mind. The earth needs your awakening in order to become healed. It needs healthy, conscious and reborn human Beings in order to lift up and regain its strength.

It is your assignment, you have made a decision for it and now it is up to you let this decision become reality.

The earth needs your loving energies. Without your love there is no growth. And your love unfolds as soon as you are purified and released. As soon as all deceptions have gone from you. And as soon as you are linked to your home.

To be reborn and to unfold your power and beauty for the benefit of human Beings and of planet Mother Earth.

This path is preordained and each deviation from it slows down the process of your healing and the recovery of earth.
But nothing can stop this process!

Certainly we will all find each other, with our Father in Heaven, with the Source of all Sources, the Love from Oneness.

Many human Beings are currently being prepared toward their permanent rebirth. Several others receive further schooling and will be guided to this awareness at a later time.

But ALL human Beings will enter the Kingdom of God.
Nobody will be forgotten!

Beloved Children of Humanity, I am JESUS SANANDA,
Accept what is given to you, because God's Capricorn pores itself out over you beyond all measures.

I am always with you. Your open heart is my home.
Go there and free yourself from all illusions.
You will be reborn.

Through your love the earth will again become a place of beauty, and she will blossom in harmony and joy.

I am with you — all days.

Honored Reader,

Since the Council of Nicaea (325) and the Council of Constantinople (381) Human Beings are being told the made up story that JESUS died on the cross. Since then, year after year, the same lie, year after year the one cross and year after year millions of human Beings take up this cross in order to do as their Lords do, according to the church history canon, the guideline of the whole Christian church. And already Medici-Pope LEO X (1475-1513) knew:
"How much the fable of Christ has helped us and ours, is well known." And it is necessary to counteract decisively against this "fable" until human Beings are liberated from this cross that has been put on them by the church.

JESUS *never was on the cross nor died on the cross!*

This is the message that needs to be spread — especially at the time of Easter. Now when suffering is prayed to and the pain is being honored, as it thereby deals like an attribute of the light or a Yoke that God put on us. The "walk of the cross" or the "death on the cross" are equally made up and the Roman Catholic Church can only exist due to this lie.

It is mandatory to tell this truth and to repeat it, until it captured the farthest corner of this earth, because:

1600 years of lies only to spread fear and make human Beings compliant are enough!

"One needs to repeat the truth over and over again, because fallacies also are preached to us over and over again, and yet not from single ones, but from the masses. In newspapers and encyclopedia, in the schools and universities, everywhere fallacy is on top, and it feels well and comfortable, in the feeling of the majority that is on its side."
JOHANN WOLFGANG GOETHE (1749-1832)

Therefore I have decided to publish, also during this year's time of fasting and time of Easter, individual chapters, which describe the actual events in Jerusalem of those days, from the books "The Biography of Jesus Part I and Part II", in the Lichtwelt-Portal.

These books were transmitted to me by JESUS SANANDA in the years 2008 and 2010 and since then all human Beings who are open to the truth, can also experience the truth.

Foremost the unmistakable word from JESUS SANANDA himself, who clearly and healingly bears witness to his "days in Jerusalem" and clearly takes a position against the greatest fallacy of the Catholic History writings:

"My Death on the Cross never happened!"

With these publications I wish foremost those readers, to whom these and additional facts are new, joy, healing and awareness.

In Love
JAHN J KASSL

THE CRUCIFIXION

I am JESUS CHRIST and I greet you, dear Children of the Earth.

It is a wonderful time you live in and all who decide to let go of their limitations awaits eternal bliss.

Today I will give you some news regarding my life on earth, so that you can let go of some old beliefs, so that these hindrances will leave you and you attain a clear vision.

As it was said in the beginning, I was never crucified nor did I die on the cross. What has really happened and how was it at that time?

The disturbances in Jerusalem increased and reached their peak. The ruling religious Priesthood saw in me an agitator, because I guided human Beings into their self-responsibility and self-love. The Priesthood saw in it an attack on their systems. They were no longer certain of their power and were afraid that human Beings would turn away from traditions, customs, rituals, sacrifices and prepared prayers.

They divined that free human Beings would no longer have the need to give themselves to preordained patterns. It was quite clear that a turning away from the then dominating religious imprints would happen, as soon as human Beings understood which origin they really come from. As soon as they direct their sight above and as soon as they step into direct contact to God, our Father. Any "go-between" role and blind faith end, as soon as this would happen. And the current Priesthood had this fear. One created a public mood against me and tried to portray me as a danger to the Roman Ruler ship.

They just could not find anything against me and repeatedly the interventions of the power-hungry Priesthood were repelled.

Wherever I was I spoke of Love, from giving, of honor, of self worth and from the Father in Heaven. Even the Jewish law could not find anything against me. But they were afraid of the results if human Beings were to wake up.

Every year a great mass of human Beings gathered in Jerusalem for the feast of Passover. So it was also then. There were disturbances prior and small riots from the Zealots were put down by the Roman army. The Zealots were a group of human Beings who demanded disentanglement from Rome and complete independence. Thereby any means were right and over years there were always brutal fights and battles.

The atmosphere in those days was heated and in this mood I was arrested the day before the festivity. I knew what was ahead of me, so I was composed and calm as they picked me up and led me into the palace of the Pontius PILATUS.

There was never betrayal, from whomever.

The Roman soldiers could find me quite easily. We were at that location quite often and it was known that I could be found there. On that evening my brothers were with me and we talked about God's Love and about his omnipresence, even if it doesn't always seem that way. Many times my friends were discouraged in this time and so I gave them new thoughts and the feeling of trust.

So I was arrested that evening in order to appease the religious guardians of the law. All means were used to portray me as a danger for peace and security. And on that evening it seemed that the scribes had their success. But this one lasted for a very short time.

I was immediately summoned to PILATUS and he "interviewed" me. It wasn't an interrogation; it was more of a conversation.

PILATUS: What side are you on?

I: On the side of the Almighty.

PILATUS: What do you think about us, the Romans?

I: It is dark at night and lite during the day. God's will is fathomless.

PILATUS: (he offers me fruit, I decline.) What do the priests have against you?

I: Ask them, did you do this?

PILATUS: Yes, they say you create unrest.

I: Do I violate the laws?

PILATUS: Nothing came to my ears. Tell me, what do you believe they have against you?

I: In the scripture is written: "He will return and will save human Beings." But they did not recognize him. Their closed hearts do not understand.

PILATUS: And what does that mean?

I: I am, who I am. And I teach unconditional Love. Transform your hearts and open yourselves. War and hate is in the hearts and if these have disappeared from it, there will be no more. Nowhere. Transform your hearts.

71

PILATUS: Do you love the Romans?

I: How could I do otherwise than to love those, who my
           Father in Heaven also loves.

PILATUS: There is no danger coming from you.
           (He gets restless and lets me taken away.)

I spend that night in the palace of the KING OF JUDEA. I sleep on a
rock and a blanket keeps me warm. It is a restless night and outside
I constantly hear agitated human Beings.

As it gets light I am picked up and released. Later it turned out
that several arrests were made during the night. Among them also
a man called SIMON THE ZEALOT who following his incorrectly
understood assignment begins the walk to the cross.

The fixed imagination that only through physical death, this
sacrifice, salvation happens, caused in SIMON that he subjected
himself to this dynamic of the events the evening before Passover
according to today's time keeping. We knew each other well and
talked about it, but it was unavoidable.

The established Jewish nomenclature was furious that I was again
free. They had assumed my death and have mixed up SIMON'S
death with mine. It was impossible for them to recognize who
indeed carried the cross, because the riotous crowd, the unrest and
also the partially disfigured body of SIMON, because of the torture,
did not allow for it.

The events somersaulted and in the chaos of the preparations
for the festivity, the many people, the constant unrest and the
controversy between the Zealots and the Romans, one easily lost the
overview.

Among many convicts SIMON THE ZEALOT was also crucified on that day.

In all this turmoil many believed for many days that I had died on the cross. But I went into retreat and conferred with my Father. I knew that also my time had come to say good-bye. Sooner or later the ruling Priesthood would succeed in my removal. In addition my heart told me it was time to depart, because my actions and being in Jerusalem were fulfilled.

A great seed has been sowed.
And this seed rises now. 2000 years after and still in the Now.

So be relaxed and in calm, beloved human child.
With all that you see, anger and pain, especially in that region[1].
These are irrevocably the last wars and the hate will go — for eternity.

The seed rises.

So be it, my Love is always with you.
JESUS CHRIST

---

1   *Near East, remark by the Author.*

BECOME LIKE CHILDREN

"...become like children so that you may enter the Kingdom of God."

I welcome you, my beloved human Child.
Your love changes everything.
Accept it and be, who you are.

I am Jesus SANANDA and your love awakens as soon as you live out
of your Being.

So what does it mean to be like children? Observe them and you
will find out. No ulterior motive, the unconditional dedication to the
moment, the instance — the Now. Their honesty so that quite often
if frightens many adults.

For a child there is no tomorrow or yesterday. Everything is in the
NOW and the instant is lived in this beauty.

Until the 7th year this authenticity is fully retained, as they are not
befallen by impairments by the environment. After that a human
Being fully takes on their karmic sheathing again and their actions
take on a different context. Normally at that age schooling also
begins and the preparations for life as you are told by society.

But what kind of preparation is this?
What do you call life?
Is it not that a forceful suffocation of feelings and the childlike
expression are the result of it?
Are your schools truly a preparation and for what?

It is not difficult to recognize that you are supposed to be formed according to the wishes of society, so that you function well in the world far from love, and lift egotism to the center of your awareness, to prevail against competition. Yet these are always your close friend, your fellow man, your brother and your sister. Instead of oneness and the feeling of togetherness, to strengthen commonness you are taught the ego-centered view of life.

And the beginning of this misfortune is set in your schools. There you grow up to a functioning part of society and your consciousness falls into deep sleep.

Before you realize it this life has passed and when you wake up at the other side of the veil, a deep pain pierces through you because you have recognized what kind of illusion was presented to you. And again you go there in order to make another attempt in order to look beyond the veil on this level of Being, so that you may return into the arms of our Father for eternity.

If you haven't already been educated by your parents and the immediate environment in that direction, with the school your path away from you finally begins and into this so painful "reality" of life on earth.

Gradually you lose and forget these wonderful qualities of feeling, which were given to you as a child. The joy, the laughter, the crying, the being in peace with oneself and the world, to live in the Now, not to worry about tomorrow and yesterday — in frankness and with love of life. You begin to plan and rack your brain. Life suddenly gets complicated and you try to protect yourself. You become anxious and finally you step out of the Now, into the stagnant energy of past and future.

Your fears and worries, all the unsolved problems and conflicts appear, and you are far from your child-like experience of daily life.

Often you think that you are responsible and you like to take on this fallacy from the collective consciousness of human Beings.

To have the heart of a child and use the mind of an adult that is what is called for.

Responsibility means first to give you an answer, about the questions of your existence on earth, about the whys and the wherefores.

Do you know these answers?
Are they taught in the schools?
Do you learn to ask the right questions?

What all distinguishes you and with what kind of template of you are you satisfied. What is needed is to return to your trust and to your responsibility. To live with pure intention and an open heart:

To find back to the magic of the moment, because each day takes care of itself.

To attain God's trust and trust in God also always means trust in self. Because *You* and *He* are one.

Most children live in this intimacy. They do not worry about tomorrow and yesterday is long gone. If you ask a child about what happened a week ago, it would be difficult for them to give you an answer. It is because in the meantime so many moments have accumulated so that the memory of them simply is not there.

The full energy of a child is oriented toward the Now. If they cry it is heart breaking and their pain is absolute.

If they are happy and you hear them laugh it is so contagious, full of happiness and of unquestioning nature. All of their "moments" are absolutely lived expressions of their Being. Nothing hinders them and is hidden or is held back.

Later you forget this, and you become controlled and calculating. The ego gains the upper hand and only rarely breaks the power of a child through you.

Many therapies have this as their goal, to bring you back to your self-awareness. They want to bring forth your feelings so you may feel better and be liberated from pain of whatever kind.

The recovery of the childlike nature in you is needed, because your plans and calculations always lead to the same result: Disappointment, because your blueprint is not aligned with your ego-dominated expectations. As soon as you detach from your childlike intensity of feelings, you lose the connection to your life plan — your blueprint.

Your original life plan does not correspond to the self-created life plan. And your expectations and plans bring the disappointment, because they do not agree with your assignments and your potential for awareness that you want to implement in this life.

It is necessary to regain this link in order to live in harmony and with your Self. In order to know who you are, where you have to be when and what your mission is. GOD has given you your mission and you have cooperated in the development of the plan before you were born.

The oblivion of these facts makes you into an anxious being yet as you are of unlimited greatness and each one is a unique image of GOD. The oblivion of your childlike nature, of your feeling of the moment and of your pure heart, brings you all this suffering.

Do you ask a child what it wants to do next week you will not receive an answer. Do you ask what happened last week they will only shrug their shoulders.

What is now is important.
In full trust that the parents care for everything they do not worry about anything.

Therefore you should also turn your heart in full trust to Father/ Mother in Heaven. He/she always cares for you, in every second of your life on earth.

Trust and do not worry. Live the day and wake up in the Now.
Because each moment has something ready for you.
If you wait for the great changes and events, you will overlook all the little miracles which come into your daily life, as they may happen in front of your eyes and until then make "great" miracles possible.

Children do not have these worries, therefore become like them.

If you live this genuine beauty of a childlike heart, you are always connected with your home. Your life in the here and now fully agrees with your blueprint and your coming fulfills itself.

Even then I tried to lead human Beings to this truth. Yet many did not understand or not correctly. And over the years the need for "being like a child" was suppressed or was dismissed as childish lack of seriousness. The word "childish" demonstrates this fallacy.

Now this image that I used had a flaw and it was no longer desirable to become like a child. Finally nobody wants to be childish and this devaluation had its effects. Far from true understanding no appropriate importance was no longer given to it and human Beings were kept in their blindness.

It is a popular trick of the rulers on earth to reinterpret, to twist or ridicule all words, which lead human Beings to the core of their Being. Thereby the mindfulness gets lost and the deep sleep in darkness finds its continuation.

Therefore I bring the Light back to you and again touch your hearts so that you wake up and ascend. So that you get up and heal your hearts in the divine Light. So that you may liberate yourself from the dominance of the ego. And so you finally recognize who you are.

In order to experience *your* beauty, in order to face *your* countenance. Thereby you enter the Kingdom in Heaven.
It spreads in *your* heart.

There the inner child blossoms and you feel like reborn.

The Kingdom of Heaven is in you and everything is in your hearts.

Become like children.
You are reborn and awaken, ascending from a deep sleep in the twilight.

I am here and illumine the path for you.
Trust and do not worry.
All is being cared for.

I am JESUS CHRIST,
My Love is always with you.

STIGMATA

The false assumption about my death on the cross has dammed up so much energy that it had to manifest.

FRANCESCO DE ASSISI, THERESA OF KONNERSREUTH or PADRE PIO have taken on the suffering of human Beings and have not confirmed my suffering. The universal belief of human Beings found its expression in their Stigmata. Not as a confirmation of my death on the cross but because of a false imagination about my death on earth.

The thoughts have a tremendous power. And there are great souls who can incorporate these powers and bundle all these energies in them like a channel, so that the ones, who adhere to certain ideas, may find relief. It is a pure service of love for human Beings.

Each stigmatized human Being through their communion with God and due to the love of their heart has absorbed the energies of innumerable human Beings and that is how the "miracle" of the Stigmata happened.

Over and over again great souls are sent to earth in order to channel these forces so that an arrest in suffering may be hindered.

It may look like these wound marks may strengthen the suffering, yet on an energetic level the opposite is the case. In order to lessen the collective experience of suffering, these wound marks have manifested themselves in a few individuals up to now. As soon as you released all of your suffering within yourself this work is no longer necessary from your Light siblings.

Everything that is not in you does not exist!

As soon as the collective energy pattern of humanity repels suffering the energy field of the planet changes. The earth will regain its peace, the joy, its beauty and the love of all creatures.

There is no further need for suffering. The power of an idea and the belief in a picture bring forth facts. Please separate and redeem yourself from suffering. That is how you change the facts.

Human Beings immersed in and interlaced with pure divine consciousness have relieved you of what was mirrored in your thoughts and your religious ideas, so that relief may happen to you.

But now it is necessary to step into your self-responsibility. Liberate yourself from your suffering. And step out of the world of the collective pity, the oppressive feeling of impotence.

Suffering is not meant for you, beloved child of mankind. Understand this truth and release yourself from it. "Nobody will/shall suffer more than I". Representatives of the Roman Catholic Church voice this figure of speech.

But this is not true, my beloved brothers and sisters. Each suffering is absolute. And each human Being is fully immersed in his suffering. The pain is unbearable and the awareness reduces itself to the situation that evoked it. There is no scale of 1 to 10. When you experience suffering, and it is filled with pain, you reach your limits.

Naturally I sensed also in my life on earth the pain of separation from my Father in Heaven. Even though I was constantly connected with Him, there were moments of pain and the suffering of my silent and eternal longing for my home. Beyond that I did not encounter any suffering.

All the events of that time had a deep "logic" and were according to the divine plan.

I was aware that I fulfilled my assignments and that the events, whatever drama they always brought forth, were in unison with my life and the will of my Father in Heaven.

But it is true I saw so much suffering.
The poor ones and the depressed ones, the enslaved ones without hope and full of anger, the burdened ones and the ill ones, trying to maintain their earthly securities at any cost. I was offered a picture full of suffering and pain.

Therefore I came to relieve the pain, in order to free human Beings from their suffering. By talking of love, joy and peace; and by carrying my Light into the hearts of human Beings.

True suffering happens as you live in darkness and at that time many did not see the Light. I had plenty of it and I gave wherever I could and where it seemed appropriate. I lived in Light. And therefore there was no suffering for me, and no pain. Where there is light there is also love. And love is always free of feelings and energies of that kind.

Please free yourselves from the idea that I had to suffer.
Liberate yourselves from this guilt even though it was for a long time presented to you as reality.

I have come in order to relieve your suffering and not in order to experience my own suffering, and in order to liberate you from suffering, not in order to create suffering in me.

Suffering does not create love, only more suffering, lack of understanding and hate.

My love is a sign for the fact that I repel suffering, it is alien to me and in my Light it dissolves, is transformed and rises up — as a divine spark into eternity.

Let go of this idea and you will be able to meet me more directly. Thereby my true message will spread in your heart.

Suffering is not designated for you and any pain you create through your thinking and your actions. Be careful in everything that you do, with every thought, with all your words, which you speak and be mindful of your deeds. Thereby you create your own reality.
You are the creator of your world. And through your loving actions infinite beauty and peace can grow.

The Heaven on earth.

Recognize this and transform your pain, your suffering, so that you may be purified and be full of light a true brother, a true sister, to your fellow human Beings.

But how can you escape from this spiral?
Whereby you do not identify yourself with "your" suffering.

And how do you do this when I hurt all over and I am full of pain all over, I hear you ask yourself?
By remembering who you are.
By understanding what has brought you here.
By recognizing your assignments.

And in the fulfillment of your assignments there is no suffering, because everything happens in harmony with your own eternal Being. You are aware of your origin.

But how do I recognize my assignments and my origin?

Have you ever asked for it?
Have you written YOUR letter to God?
Did you fill your heart full of longing and have posed your questions?
How unconditionally are you interested in your history?
Are you ready to let go in order to learn, to recognize and to
experience of who you really are?

Often times I spoke in parables and there the idea of "giving up" was
talked about.

"... go there, sell everything and follow me..."

Thereby the letting go is meant.
This moves you forward, toward you and away from suffering.

This is not meant verbatim, but also that could be the case. Here it
means the "selling all" is the readiness to give all in order to receive
the awareness of your Being. To separate yourself from everything,
in order to gain everything; thereby your full attention is needed
and any binding comes from you.

So that you may be free when you encounter me. This encounter is
always an experience of God and brings you into the knowledge of
your power and strength.

All bindings to this reality dissolve from the inside.
Often there were human Beings who took these words verbatim, sold
everything and even then were still plagued by suffering and pain.
Transformation happens in you and transforms your heart.

The fullness is necessary and is meant for you, but you should not be
attached to anything — this is the freedom of which I talked about
and this is the meaning of selling everything — not to be attached to
anything in order to be present in the moment.

It does not require any stigmata for you to redeem your suffering. It happens as you ask your questions and you begin to listen to your inner voice.

If you arrive in your love then you walk in my steps.
It is always the love that removes everything from you, the suffering, the worry and the fear, in order to give you ALL — the eternal entry into your true essence.

Let go of your suffering and you will also not find it in this world. It will dissolve, like the fog dissolves as soon as the sun breaks through.

Your suffering is the suffering of your fellow human Beings.
Your joy is there joy.

Nails through my hands do not exist.
No blood and no death on the cross.

Liberate yourself from this belief even if it is difficult for you.

Put the invocation in this book into your hand, go into your chamber and I am with you.

Ask your questions and I will give you an answer.
Have patience and let it happen.
Open your heart to me. And all wounds will close.

What remains, is your divinity, your light and your love.

Your Being as it is.
Your essence — God.

I am with you, all days.
JESUS SANANDA

THE PURE HEART

"Blessed are the pure in heart, for they will see God."

Beloved Child of God,

Are you aware of its significance? Do you realize how important it is to be in your heart? Are you ready to take this step?

In all the chapters you find a central red thread and you notice that it is always the heart we are dealing with. Your return to the core of your Being. Freed from all blindness you have direct access into your sanctuary.

It is about your heart, because from it you create ALL and each insight has its origin there.

A pure heart is perfection.
Such a heart emits only love; it is incapable of anything else.

Such a human Being is awakened, reborn and has entered the Kingdom of God. Truly, such a human Being has shed all limitations and is aware of his origin. No deception can blind him, neither fear nor worry meddle in his consciousness. The kingdom of heaven that he experiences is omnipresent and out of this awareness he accomplishes his share in Creation.

A pure heart only knows a single intent.
The intent of unconditional love. A pure heart is always in the center, in the middle and no situation can disturb it.

To have a pure heart means that you have arrived, means that you have seen and says that you have entered into the eternal essence of the Father.

You awake gradually and there are a few among you who have found, have entered into Heaven. Who have seen and yet remain among you. They are the carriers of the Light in order to illumine the path for you and daily there are more.

This development can no longer be stopped. The earth again becomes harmonious and is brought into unison with Creation. Automatically human Beings rise up in order to experience peace, freedom, joy and love. The old can go and the dynamic is truly awe-inspiring.

Never in the evolution of mankind has such a collective longing been developed. On all levels of Being more and more human Beings decide to finally recognize who they are. The efforts and your intentions are clear and thereby this new earth, this new mankind, grows up.

We from the spiritual level observe this with great joy and there is a great mystery in it, how and when the "critical point" will be reached. The point at which human Beings as a collective wake up in consciousness, fully visible to all.

The point that withdraws all energies from any destructivity, any lie, every fear, each manipulation, every worry, every misuse of power and any lack of love.

But so much is already certain from our point of view:

There will be remarkable changes and those, who now still think them safe and continue their game of power, violence and hate, will overnight step down from the stage, which they dominated for many centuries.

The "critical point" will be reached very soon. And be happy that an earth of peace, tolerance, understanding and oneness will be born. You will live in unison with Creation and will cooperate with nature.

All destructions and exploitation will end and very soon a fully new consciousness will be established. What for so long has been waited for is now being fulfilled. Human Beings return home. And your hearts will become pure and will become a temple of Light.

Also your bodies change and your DNA will again become complete. Based on this process you become aware of your divinity and thereby attain knowledge of your Being and about how everything is related to each other and joined together.

We see that you long for it very much. This intent, this longing is the energy, which brings the transition. You can count the days and the end of earth, as you have known it so far, is near.

But please do *not* be afraid!

The events will have a toned down form because the light energy of your hearts directly affects these changes on earth.
Be free of worry and fear.

God's hand spreads out over the whole earth. We, Light Beings from beyond the veil, are always here and our service does not fail.

Trust, whatever may come. Go there on your path to the heart. Until you have arrived and have entered.

The purity of your heart is the basis upon which the whole earth heals. Thereby life encounters love and thereby you experience it. You are in the process to create Heaven on earth. And every human Being who participates in it affects immeasurable things.

The trees carry plenty of fruits and the seed comes forth. We are all connected with each other and you now become aware of that fact.

The connection to the spiritual world has been established and again it is possible to make the invisible visible. The transformation affects this and it is a gift that you offer to yourself.

The light carriers among you gain in strength and soon one will not be able to withdraw from their power. Hesitant, fearful and unbelieving ones will have to make a decision, because that day is close. Very close.

It is the "day of judgment", yet this day has no date, because these decisions are made in the hearts of human Beings, everybody on his own and at the optimum time.

Aren't there many such days, because doesn't each human Being have his "day of judgment"? It is the day of salvation, the awareness and enlightenment.

The day of the full acceptance of your power, the day of your return, the day of your acceptance in the circle of the eternally loving ones.

Therefore it is your pure heart that puts down this last bridge.
The bridge into oneness.

While you walked through time for centuries, in your heart the mustard seed grew into a gorgeous bloom of life. You became the bloom, the leaf, the branch, you are the root and the fruit — the tree. And now you begin to understand and recognize what secret life held ready for you.

Your service on earth comes to an end and the attainment of a pure heart is the sign for it.

Yet before that there is still reason to celebrate, because you return Mother Earth to its place in Creation. And as soon as the dark clouds, which still move over the earth today, have been dissolved, you will recognize your countenance in God's eternal Light.

Walk these last steps with mindfulness, with a clear spirit and with dedication. A pure heart will guide you.

"Blessed are the pure in heart..."

Thereby you bless your fellow human Beings and Mother Earth. Everything is connected with each other.

"... because they will see God."

From face to face.
And again you recognize your image.

Thereby all of you enter the eternal Kingdom of God in Heaven — and where you are is Heaven, because God's Kingdom is omnipresent.

With this message I say goodbye for today.
Thereby my beloved JAHN will also get some rest.[2]

Adonai, I am amongst you.
JESUS SANANDA

---

2   *Jesus makes a joke, because he knows that today I was supposed to have a "free" day. The past days a lot has been transmitted and therefore I was expecting a pause. Despite the great fulfillment that is inherent in such a work, naturally there is also tiredness – and I am used that my companions from the spiritual world know every stir in me. Besides, this final remark shows that humor is also important and that the spiritual world, but especially Jesus, posses a good portion of it. (Remark of the Author.)*

INVOCATION

I ask you, Jesus Christ, to transform my ideas of suffering and guilt through your Light. I ask you for your presence and for your Light of Love.

I am now ready to let go and to recognize that my joy, my peace, my kindness and my love are the powers, which blossom now.

I am ready to separate myself from all distressed thoughts, the pain-filled feelings about your demise on earth.

Please cut now the energetic bonds so that I may face your countenance.

I recognize you as the one you are.
As my brother, who shows me my own beauty and accompanies me during the now upcoming journey, back to God.

I am *now* ready to let go of *all* suffering!
I am free of any guilt and of pain.
I am who I am!
Love, Peace, Joy and Happiness.
God's eternal Light.

Beloved Jesus, I thank you.
My Heart is eternally joined with your Heart.
I am that I am!
In Eternity, Amen.

LOVE YOUR NEIGHBOR

Welcome beloved Child of God and I greet you, my Love is with you and all days I accompany you wherever you may be. Unfold your wings and experience your infinity, here on earth in the eternal Now-Time.

I am JESUS CHRIST and again I give you a new perspective about my life on earth so that you can liberate yourself from all the adopted and often inappropriate pictures about my life in Jerusalem.

Today we dedicate ourselves to love and how it can be implemented in your daily life, even though you feel surrounded by very weakening and hate-filled energies.

"...love your neighbor as yourself."

This is my clear and always valid message. Given at that time and today I renew this one and truly it is imperative to let this life quality resurrect. In case you succeed, you are therefore asked to look inside yourself again. Into your inner world, into your heart and into your Being.

Then you will find everything and you search will be crowned with the insight about your all-embracing ability — to love.

So begins your journey to you based on you looking inside and with the fact that you turn all of your attention to the inner; and you see your whole totality of love.

Everything begins in you because you must learn to know yourself in order to love.

You gain your self-love by beginning to accept what constitutes you. To recognize your shadows always means to take another step toward love. To learn to love yourself with all your "faults" and fears, with the inadequacies and also with the often long unnoticed and dammed up energies in you.

Feelings of fury, anger, worry, fear and impotence come forth, even though the feeling of hate can spread. And while you observe all this, you love yourself. You do not reject this side of you, because it belongs to you and this attitude affects dissolution.

You gain a loving look at your patterns, ideas and your lack of courage. You discover that God loves you like you are right now. In this moment while torturing thoughts and emotions haunt you.

On the path to your salvation you make the acquaintance with your inner "monsters" and you are not afraid anymore.

I am there and whenever you call on me, I will come in order to help you in the resolution of these feelings, which call for salvation.

All it takes is your courage, beloved child of mankind, so that you may look at it and free yourself. This courage brings you into your heart and gradually you let go of fear and you begin — to love yourself.

Slowly the feeling dawns on you that is God who loves you, and the more you dissolve your hindering thoughts and emotions, the more understanding you become in your look at your fellow human Beings. Because then nothing human is unfamiliar to you anymore and you understand the actions and the intentions of human Beings. You look through their motivation, because you have met yourself and you can surmise what it is all about the destructive energies.

Thereby you become understanding and even-tempered.

Your soft heart recognizes and is full of sympathy for those who have not attained this insight about their true nature. Your rebellion against the inner "enemy" is gone. You are free and this freedom is the fertile soil for your love.

Before you can truly love your neighbor, you must therefore learn to love yourself at first. Without self-love the brotherly love will not work.

To accept yourself fully and totally. Totally uncompromising. Whatever you discover in your heart, to accept it in love and then let it go if it hinders you to love.

Also your pain is in need of your love.
Also your wounds call for the Light and the loving power in you. Truly it is easy to love somebody who loves you and returns your love. To love where there is love succeeds by itself and this feeling fills you completely.

But to love where there is darkness, where there is fear and hate, is a true challenge, but necessary if you want to regain your wholeness. In order to love where hate is, you must have looked at your own hate, your inner subversion and inner desperation and anger. After that what is needed is reconciliation and not to judge or condemn these feelings.

Do not cast judgment over you and you will not speak in judgment over your fellow human Beings.

In the experience of your own desperation you understand the desperation of others and by looking at your own abyss your heart opens in order to understand your brother and your sister.
In order to meet in true understanding also of their needs and fears, expressed by loveless behavior.

"...do not condemn so that you may not be condemned."

Everything is connected with each other and if you do not judge, you also begin to see your fellow human Beings in a new light. Until you have gone through the valley of tears and have seen whose child you are, it does not even occur to you any longer to judge, because your heart overflows with full sympathy and love for your siblings.

Because each human Being is your brother, each human Being is your sister.

Without exception. All human Beings are joined through an invisible inner umbilical cord. The direct connection to all of us Father and Mother in Heaven.

This one source has brought forth everything and born it. And therefore we all are always connected with each other. Visible and invisible, but always linked to each other through this bond of love to our home, to our assignments, to our prime force in the universe.

As soon as you arrange your inner world and you accept yourself, it is over with judgments and condemnations. You attain the power of distinction, but assessments of any kind have lost their importance.

Everything begins from you, in you and with you. If you love yourself, if you accept yourself, then you can easily assume that we meet on the outside.

You recognize yourself in it and like with a mirror you sense this reflection as soon as you meet with whom, where and however. You know the connections and due to your power of distinction is it possible for you to feel inside and to look into human Beings. You see their pain and desperation.

You know where it is coming from and you recognize their broken hearts. Therefore your sympathy and your kindness awaken, because you have recognized that only these forces can bring healing.

You have experienced it yourself:
As soon as you have accepted yourself, the pain became less and your love grew to a lushly sprouted itself giving away bloom from your heart.

Now you succeed to recognize the desperation of your brother from the viewpoint of your awakened heart and your love can be felt, your heart exudes this strength and your brother absorbs this energy.

The hearts of human Beings are all equal in their core. And the pure energy of heart's love will be instantly recognized and felt.
Your dedication and your sympathy change the hearts of human Beings and it is obvious that love has an incredible power in it.

You love unconditionally and it shows!
Your example moves human Beings to the exploration of their inner beauty.

And it is always an example that brings a change. Not words without deeds. It is your Being that visibly affects your environment.

Therefore it is urgently necessary that you reconcile with yourself on the inner and you find your self-love.

"...because you will recognize them in their deeds."

That is the point. A human Being in the awareness of his strength and power, a human Being, whose love is awakened, has a great radius and directly affects the hearts of fellow human Beings. Many are ready to be touched by this energy in order to find their strength of love.

Your example is the one that counts. No empty words and not the Sunday sermon. It is the deeds coming from a purified and pure heart, which let the earth become what it is: An eternal place of God's beauty.

You were at the beginning and you are now. You are God and HE is you. Everything is connected and comes from the oneness of Being.

Your redeemed heart knows that, your purified heart is the messenger of this fact and wherever you may be, your love pours out as an all joining and healing power.

Human Beings long so much for it, yet many have lost belief in it. The belief that it is indeed possible to bring forth a new earth. With all the attributes, which enrich living together and which make love the only reality.

They have lost the confidence, because they see what happened around the globe and they do not know how one can ever stem these doings.

The solution also for it is always — in you.
YOUR LOVE IS ABLE TO DO ALL.

Initially take on yourself so that you can love yourself. Redeem your issues and free yourself from the slavery of your thoughts, ideas and emotional blockages.

You begin to love yourself as you are and as God also loves you.
You begin to see your beauty and this picture will also become visible to your fellow human Beings.
This is the first and most important step!
Due to this self-experience you bring forth just by itself a lifestyle that enables your siblings to regain their own power.

Your example begins to work.

Maybe you will be asked whereby you have come into this awareness of life and what made you so confident in this time? Do not impose on others but talk about it in an appropriate manner. But what always counts, are the deeds.

You will be observed and many will see that your love brings forth more love and therefore they become aware of their own abilities and power. Be patient and trust your Father in Heaven. Everything takes its time and thus awareness is not born over night.

Your heart recognizes and you know from your own experience that everything takes its place in God's order.

Your self-love is the key to the hearts of human Beings. Only thereby love of your neighbor becomes possible. The acceptance of your Being is the way in order to be without judgment and to act in kindness out of a loving heart. And your deeds create this new reality.

I have come to give an example.
Now go there and give your example so that a collective awakening of human Beings, a permanent anchoring of the energy of love and mankind living in oneness may become reality.

Let nothing be untried and do justice to your assignment.

We from the spiritual world accompany you and each human Being is supported and accompanied by us in infinite love.

Exercise your responsibility.

Again I have returned and I am among you.
Project "Earth" finds its completion.

Of the "days of judgment" there are many in order to find enough opportunities and be able to ascend. This means to always accept your reality. It is your rebirth as Loving-Self.

It is: *Your merger with the wellspring of All-That-Is.*

I am JESUS SANANDA and I am here, all days.
Your heart knows me.

THE RESURRECTION

Beloved Children of the Light,

I am always with you and whenever you call on me, I am there, among you.
I am JESUS CHRIST and the transformation is far advanced:
"No rock will remain upon another."

The changes are truly honorable.
The earth is constantly raised in its vibration field and thereby you regain your consciousness. Thereby you are automatically brought up to your true Being.

Today we would like to turn our attention to the resurrection. It is a mystery that until today searches for true understanding.
What is meant, when we talk about the resurrection?

Certainly not the physical resurrection and any imagination of it are inappropriate. Please consider that you incarnated in innumerable bodies during innumerable lives and it is not intended in Creation that these bodies and life shells resurrect. You always incarnate in a body, yet it is your spirit that breathes life into this expression. As soon as your body has done its service, it finishes its work and dies. Your eternal spirit escapes and you find yourself again on the spiritual level of Being.

This is how it has happened life after life and resurrection of your body does not exist. Therefore it is important to gain clarity on this subject, who you are and to become aware of your eternal Being behind it. Your spirit is immortal and your consciousness knows it.

Become aware of Self and you will live in Eternity.

Now you were kept in ignorance for centuries and one liked to let you believe that physical resurrection is the crowning achievement. The "day of judgment" served as dramaturgical background, and thereby you were denied the awakening and the actual *resurrection into your power.*

Furthermore, you were injected with fear and guilt feelings; and the subservience against the establishment became the norm. In exchange you were promised your reward in Heaven and with the resurrection of the body this was supposed to fulfill itself.

No, my beloved brothers and sisters of the Light.
These false prophets let you believe for centuries that my resurrection of the body happened and thereby a "reality" was put in front of you, which robbed you of the freedom to communicate with your spirit and your heart.

Your trust in your God-Being and your knowledge about the eternal existence of your spirit thereby faded gradually. You became sluggish, fearful and driven by the constant worry of your naked survival of your body on earth; and you forgot who you are.

The dogma of the physical resurrection substantially contributed to the fact that human Beings so willingly subordinated themselves to the demands of the manipulative forces. After all everything will be readjusted after death due to the resurrection and any suffering will be rewarded and honored.

You have waited and death brought you liberation. Yet when you awakened on the side of the Light, you had to recognize that you were betrayed, because there was no resurrection.

Connected with a frequent self-denying piety you had accepted what seemed unavoidable. Thereby you became guidable and easy to be used for the intentions of the ruling cartels on earth.

This misuse has come to an end!

The truth about you, about your actual strength and power is now given to you and everywhere human Beings look through the game of those who have sat at the levers of power. Yet their power is broken and human Beings return to their self-determination.

We from the spiritual world concretely affect on it that the truth comes into the light and foremost that you find back into your heart, into the knowledge about yourself and the eternal Light of your immortal Being, your spirit and your divinity.

My resurrection, as it was already mentioned, did not happen. The women came to the grave, yet the grave was empty. They were astonished and yet they and my brothers were even more astonished, when I appeared several days later after the events about my supposed crucifixion. Without any wound marks and full of Light, because Heaven supplied me with it and my inner Being was filled with Love for human Beings.

Some could not believe that I was physically in front of them and many actually believed initially in the resurrection. My wife MIRIAM, my mother MARY and my brothers knew very soon that I did not meet death, yet the news about my "miraculous resurrection" spread across the land.

Reports, which were written down years later about the events, nurtured this legend and gradually history writing made a Divinity out of me, which corresponded to the intentions of the newly forming religious structures.

The resurrection is just as invented as the death on the cross.

To accept suffering in this life as wishful in order to harvest the fruits in Heaven was the despising of human Beings game of the dark forces. And I repeat again:

This game is irreversibly over!

Yet it exists, the resurrection. It is the becoming reborn,
the resurrecting in order to turn to one's reality.

In order to retain your divinity it requires your resurrection. The awakening in your eternal spirit, here in the now, runs into the resurrection. You are reborn and resurrected, self-confident and full of respect for yourself and your fellow human Beings.
Liberated from suffering, fear and worry.

This state of being gives false understood humbleness, desired suffering or manipulated piety no space.
You are who you are!

And this has been my message in Jerusalem and everywhere I walked. I brought light in order to ignite the lights in the often fear occupied hearts of human Beings. All the time I was filled with the knowledge of my Being and I was always aware of my origin.

This reality created a resonance in many human hearts and many realized then who they are. Yet many followed other intentions and the events of the last two thousand years have shown that Light was missing, that the hearts were closed and that this lack has brought you to the edge of destruction.

Now on the other hand the cup is full and an infinite number of human children have awakened and daily there are more.

The complete transformation of earth is ongoing.

It is the time that has been often predicted for you. This is the time of total dedication to the Light. On the spirit level you have already given your consent and increasingly this intent penetrates your day-to-day consciousness.

Therefore do not be afraid!

Mother Earth is prepared for the reinsertion into the universal order of the Creator. And your participation is important in this.

So free you from old patterns, examine carefully which belief doctrines in your energy bodies wait for dissolution. Observe your thoughts and foremost:

CALL THE LIGHT!

So that it may redeem you from all this garbage, from false programming, the ideas about the world and from the ideas about yourself.

Please, turn to your heart.

Your hearts are the true treasure chambers in you.

They know all and this knowledge guides you out of darkness and into God's Light of Love.

The love is what is needed the most right now.
Out of a loving heart flows this energy that lifts the earth and the human Being into the new reality.

Do not allow that you will be dishonored any longer.

Keep your energy body pure and do not allow that negativity, fear or dramas of any kind will unsettle you. Be aware of your strength and power.

Be cognizant of your origin.
Do not be satisfied with what the collective opinion (still) offers you.

The process of the healing of the planet cannot be stopped by anybody. Therefore do not worry, instead take your steps, because *your* participation is needed.

The resurrection of mankind into a fully conscious Being of the Galaxy is fully underway. Your rebirth into the infinite All-That-Is. God's master plan finds its fulfillment NOW.

May this information lead you to new shores, because much that seemed true until now, is untrue and much of what had been far from any reality for you, now penetrates to you and fills your hearts with joy and love. Because when you are in joy and in love you conform with your Being.

Examine your inner world, go there under *your* roof and listen to the voice in you. Everything is already there, waiting for your wake-up call in order to lift up, get up, be reborn and return to your eternal brothers and sisters in God's infinity.

Be blessed and my Love reaches unrestrictedly each heart.

See you soon, you Beloveds.
JESUS SANANDA

THE WILL OF GOD

"...even a single hair will not fall out without the Will of the Father."

Beloved children of humanity,

Today I will give you a deeper understanding about what it means to live according to the "Will of GOD".

It is an immutable fact that all of us on all levels of creation are subject to GOD'S will. Nothing develops or happens without this divine intent and therefore we are all connected with each other. Today I give you this wonderful truth again in order to deepen your understanding about it.

Therefore let us now go back to "the time" when all had its beginning — in the reality of Being in the eternal All-That-Is.

In the beginning there was GOD and all of us were HE, part of the all-encompassing reality of Love. This reality existed in ALL and truly from eternity to eternity. There was neither beginning nor time. It was and is eternally.

Let me say it somewhat simplified and as follows, that in the beginning only GOD existed in his highest expression. And all of us were this expression and dwelled in Him.

Yet GOD began to create levels of experience. And so he created the levels of being. His Light manifested very subtle, but also physical expressions of his nature. And while this happened, bustle began in the eternal oneness.

Finally began the separation and disentanglement from oneness, and the divine consciousness attained reality in dense matter. Thus the form of the planet earth became the essential realm in order to experience GOD, in order to experience oneself in dense and solid matter as divine.

For earth very special "rules" were created and the great "experiment" began:

What happens if gods distance themselves from Oneness?
How will these experiences shape the universe?

Therefore all of us were born on earth countless times and we were pushed closer and closer to the challenges, which were demanded of us.

God's will, which also was and is our will, is being realized and gradually human Beings begin to understand what great service of love they perform on earth.

All of you are Gods.

An eternal time ago you have decided to enter the dense vibration level on earth or on earth-like planets. All of you wanted to experience your divinity on this level of Creation and you have come in order to experience, to learn and to grow.

"All is God's Will."

The will is not a distant dictum, which you are supposed to subject yourself to, but it is your true freedom!
Your will and GOD'S Will are identical.
There is no separation regarding this. There is only your ignorance what your will actually is.

And the more you give yourself to the Will of GOD and to His Light, the stronger is your merger with Him, the sooner you return to your prime knowledge about your union with GOD.

It is always your ego consciousness that pretends to fall into lack of will as you choose GOD. Actually each step toward Him/You strengthens your power and your will.

Because each step brings you closer to your origin and the point of departure, which is the eternal and all allowing Will of GOD. Thereby you let go of your ego, but never your will. So do not let yourself be misled and do not give your ego this power.

"Without God you are nothing, with God all."

This is also self-explanatory, because you can only be all due to your awareness of your divinity. And without it you are nothing. Thereby your ego consciousness can suggest whatever it may.
You are nothing and you sense it in your body.
Your unrest is a sign for it.

Are you in GOD you are in you; and in you is GOD.

Your Being knows it and your ego overlays it so that it can live. Great wisdom lies in the understanding of this reality. If you make it your own you lose the chains, which hinder you to give up what your ego let you believe. Your ego consciousness has no overview and no hair will bend to its will. Yet your all-encompassing divine consciousness is powerful and all knowing.

In the eternal All-That-Is, all past, current and future situations yield to this power. You come out of this power and even more:
You are this power!

GOD'S Will and your will are, as soon as you found yourself in agreement with your primal essence, ONE. You do not have to be afraid of the steps, which lead to the dissolution of your ego, because your reward is immense.

"Do not worry about the Kingdom of God and everything else will be given to you."

The Kingdom of God is in your heart. Care about that your heart gains strength and that it becomes free of blindness. The more you succeed in this the more beautiful and the more fulfilling will be your existence. Your actions carry the signature of your heart.

And truly have you finally arrived at that point, then God's abundance will pour out over you and you will never have to thirst or your hunger will be satisfied at all times. If you walk on the path to your Father, which is always the path into your heart, then this abundance, which cares for itself, will be certain for you day in and day out. It is one of the fundamental laws in the order of the Creator that for you it is cared for.

Your life receives everything in order to unfold.
No human Being shall suffer from lack as he devotes himself to the will of the Father. Based on this devotion you will be transformed and gradually the veils will thin out and you reach the Source.

Strive for GOD'S Kingdom in you and your life will abundantly find fulfillment.

The more you worry about earthly affairs, hold on to them or even get uptight, the weaker your energy of love will flow. These blockages cause your suffering and any lack. If you give your Being into the hands of the Father in Heaven, into his trust, you will relax.

Do not worry about tomorrow. Remain anchored in the NOW and act out of your heart. The Kingdom of GOD is inside of you. Thereby you enable the Light to unfold its effect. Your energies can freely flow again and you experience GOD'S constant presence.

The signs of your devotion are the feeling, to be impotent, to be at somebody else's mercy, and to lose control.

As soon as you completely let go, the curtain opens and the harmony of your Being in all its dignity spreads out in front. Any anxiety yields, impotence becomes power. You have cognizance of the why.

Your Being experiences everything as grace, whatever your ego sensed as threat. Where your narrowed consciousness sensed trepidation, your awakened Self - experiences — liberation. Everything is turned on its head. Up is down and down is up.

The solutions to all your problems, of personal as well as global nature, lie in the retrieval of your consciousness. There is no other GOD besides you. He is in you.

Ask for the grace of this realization. Love is put into your heart for eternity and in this oneness you are again a fully conscious creation of divine order.

Please consider always that GOD'S plans are not known to you, yet they are familiar to you. Do you get close to this knowledge, and then you realize yourself as divine and in union with Father/Mother in Heaven.

There is a silent agreement between you and GOD: He fights for your love and you refuse; yet he fights until you can no longer resist his courtship and surrender to His charm. You give in and in this merger you find — you.

What is true devotion and how do you attain it?

True devotion means to die. To give in and completely let go of the ego. Like a mustard seed falls into the soil in order to carry fruits in abundance. It is the rebirth into All-That-Is.

The awakening of the heart, the death of your illusions affects this transformation.

Devotion means an unquestioning nature and trust. Your Father in Heaven cares for you. This knowledge makes you omnipresent and the ego finds no hold.

Devotion means to let go of — *All*. It is your ideas, opinions, fears, worries and doubts. Your false programming, made manifest due to many life times. You must die the last of all deaths in order to fully become of who you are.

Everything is taken care of, as you give in and this last death carries the seed of birth, your rebirth in it. In order to abundantly carry fruits, for the benefit of human Beings.

This process is carried out step by step. Until you finally recognize that you are different. Until you recognize that the seed which you have put in the soil a long time ago, grew into a shadow-giving tree.

Your devotion affects the transformation of your issues, until all is redeemed and you have completed this transformation.

You have awakened.

You are in union with all life; GOD'S Will is now your freedom. Based on this freedom you love and you emit your light. Your divinity becomes visible, and you have arrived.

Beloved children of humanity, children of the Light, all of you are of divine origin and we are all joined with each other eternally, over time and space, beyond all of your imaginations.

GOD the Father calls you back into His arms.
You have exceptionally accomplished your service of love. Be mindful and liberate yourself from the great deception of the reality considering you.

Call on us, us, the brothers and sisters who have walked ahead of you; we will be there whenever you need us in order to attain clarity. We do not need sleep!

Whenever you call, our accompaniment is certain.
In order that you may become who you are, since eternity and from the beginning of time.

Be greeted and my Love is with you everywhere, because your heart is my home.

JESUS SANANDA

EPILOG

Beloved One, GOD'S Child and eternal Light of Creation!

Liberate yourself from all limitations, which you have put on yourself!
Free yourself from all your ideas, opinions and from your emotions,
which are distressed and not appropriate! Free yourself from the
false picture that you have of me and — wake up! Become aware
and attain complete consciousness of your Being!

Free yourself from suffering that creates fear, paralyzes you and
keeps you in agony! Recognize who you really are! Grab for the
empowerment in order to reclaim your wholeness and your divinity!

Here and now. On earth, on the experience level that kept you in the
illusion of Being-separated from GOD.

Reject the fearful, suffering and paralyzing energies, which still
come into your energy field from the collective consciousness!
Please become aware what is being played and look through the
structures, which keep the earth and you human Beings in darkness
for generations!

WAKE UP!

Get up and lift your sight to the Father in Heaven!
Search for your inner core, your home and in your hearts you will
find them! Bring these qualities again to the forefront and be divine,
be perfect, be free, be kind, be clear in all that you think, what you
speak and in your actions.

Accept your *true* status!

You are an eternal and unique expression of the Creator and in your heart lays this knowledge, waiting to be raised by you. Do not let yourself be misled, neither from your ego nor from events coming to you from the outer!

"Ask and it will be given to you!"

Ask for this awareness and it will spread out in you until you will face your divinity, fulfilled, perfected and permeated by it!

I have given you this book, so that you can liberate yourself and be able to let go; in order that you recognize that love does not bring suffering; so that you understand that you can experience GOD'S glory as a human Being. Here and now, due to your perfect "Being-Human".

Meaning to bring the all-encompassing energy of love as a human Being to unfolding. You therefore accept the "Being-Human", make peace with all the fear-bringing imaginations around you — and they can go.

Therefore accept your life as it unfolds in front of you! Accept the current state of your development and awareness! Observe and stay calm, do not judge — neither yourself nor others.

Observe and let go in order to become free and regain the sight of your beauty!

Due to your Being-Human you are divine and thereby you attain the mastership on this level. Take some time for yourself, let prayer, the meditation and the devotion to GOD be a permanent part of your daily routine!

Steady observation and turning into your inner silence let you become aware and understanding. And we also, your brothers and sisters from the invisible world thereby have optimal access to you, because we can take care of you issues, which you want to redeem, focused and without distraction.

This work *must* be done now.
For every human Being on this planet.

Much happens on the level of dreams, yet not everything can find healing and realization there. The integration into your day-to-day consciousness is important, because only thereby you can radiate and bring your light to human Beings. Therefore this self-examination, the observation of your thoughts, the feelings and your deeds, is crucial, in order to fully regain your strength.

The earth is on a unique journey back to the Source, to the Father, the Mother of Creation and this process is far advanced. Therefore it is necessary that you open yourself to this process and let go of your fears. Because freedom, peace, joy and love are qualities, which can only settle down in a purified heart, meaning in a heart without fear and free from false ideas.

Please begin with your devotion to your true essence! Do not postpone it and allow yourself to look at your beauty.

I am JESUS CHRIST and all the time with you.
Any call will be heard and everywhere, where you need support, help and our loving energies, you will get them also. Please demand them!

We are always here and much closer than you guess.
Decide, begin with the "evacuation work" and let your heart be free! Release your mind from unnecessary, negative and from the collective carried over thoughts!

Release your world of feelings from emotions, which hinder you to be in Love! Release your actions from frequent false intentions, which stem from these!

Loving intentions create the kind of world you want to live in. And so it is in your hand what you manifest.

You are the creators of realities.

In this world or beyond. Your power is absolute and omnipresent. Therefore it is your intentions, your thoughts and emotions, your energies, which create reality.

Do you understand now, how important it is, to redeem your inner structures? Becoming aware through silent observation. Free of judgments and in love.

Your thoughts bring forth emotions, and the emotions determine your actions. Everything has an effect and is connected with each other.

It is in your hand to decide. To see yourself as the one you are and deny access to your Being for all destructive energies. It is up to you to think love, to feel love and to act in love. And that has an effect!

Thereby you transform the world.
Your transformation is what counts NOW.

"Knock and it will be opened for you."

I have come in order to bring you this happy message, in order to renew it and in order to guide you back into your home in Heaven. There is no need for any more suffering, pain or fear. This book can free you and open a completely new vision of life for you.

Wasn't it the imagination of sin that let you become a sinner?
And wasn't it the illusion of fear that made you into fearful creations?
Wasn't it the collective feel of suffering that brought suffering to you?
And wasn't it the pain, this sinister phantom, the reason that you
had to experience pain, as it subtly dug into your heart?
Therefore it is now Love that heals all, takes away these illusions
and liberates you from these dramas.

You are free and without sin! Everyone is born like that and each
one is pure and perfect. That is your eternal essence.

Do not let yourself be fooled! Sin brings forth suffering, pain and fear.
Be aware that you are liberated from it!

Sin is an invention of human Beings, in order to rule over other
human Beings. Thereby you remain unsure, discouraged and far
from your divinity.

*Go into your silence, recognize that, look through this deception and
become — GOD!*

Through this book joy, peace and love may enter your heart.
Therefore it is necessary that you can see my life on earth as JESUS
in this new light. The thoughts and emotions about my life and
my alleged death in Jerusalem, which were fed from the group
consciousness, had the power to paralyze you, let you live your days
lethargically and fearful.

Now this biography shall bring you salvation and healing. Thereby it
shall guide you into the awareness of your almightiness due to the
power of Love.

This first part of the biography finds its conclusion now and further
clarifications and discussions about my life as JESUS will follow.

It is time that the truth comes to light. In order to free you and take away any guilt.

Recognize who you are, *who you really are!*

Recognize your eternal substance! Create a new world, a new reality that recreates itself due to a purified heart! Over and over until a unified and in Love connected humanity becomes a reality.
Remove all separation and experience yourself as oneness!

Yet before that reclaim your greatness and become one with the Father in Heaven! The becoming one with Him/Her will create this new world.

Finally everything brings forth oneness that was born out of oneness — on all levels of All-That-Is. Everything is joined with each other.
Please honor this, illumine your heart and reclaim your almightiness, the almightiness to be GOD'S infinite expression of Light and Love!

Claim *your true heritage!*

Now I say goodbye to you, it is not a final farewell, just a quite stepping back in order to celebrate your steps toward becoming whole.
As soon as you call me, I step again forward in order to hold you, to console you and to guide you so that you progress further, further and closer to your reality; until all of us find ourselves again in the Oneness of the Father.

So be it, Now and in Eternity.

Amen.

LETTER FROM THE AUTHOR

Beloved Reader!

The "channeling" requires full attention and foremost a readiness to be free of one's own opinions and imaginations so that the light energy can flow freely and therefore a full and clear understanding of the message may be possible.

The writing of the "Jesus Biography" posed a special challenge for me to free myself from old pictures about the told and written history of JESUS'S life. This wasn't always easy, because the patterns from my childhood and my many lives, often of a catholic imprint, wanted to be redeemed. So I grew into this new perspective about the JESUS'S life on earth.

After I had written down the last chapter I received the final confirmation that this book, word for word, corresponded to the facts and that it portrays the truth about the events at that time. Much of it I could immediately and easily accept, yet others took its time.

The "interview" with PILATUS was such an issue and it took me a long time in order to gain the certainty that the encounter of JESUS with PILATUS took place in this simple, short and almost unspectacular manner. After all, I was full of pictures of JESUS'S suffering, the cross and the humiliation.

For me this book is a "joyous message" like it could not be better. Thereby the liberation from suffering may happen and the self-worth may increase.

Whatever you may experience in this book, what you accept or what you cannot accept, give yourself and the events some time.

Because so much is certain:
This is not the last revelation and much will be brought into the light on the different levels of Being.

With the joy of a richly gifted one

JAHN J KASSL
Vienna, December 2006

"A book of this time, given through God's hand.

It was reborn in the knowledge

of the Oneness of all Life.

Highest divine consciousness is reborn

and accompanies human Beings

again on Earth."

JAHN J KASSL

THE AUTHOR

JAHN J KASSL, born in 1965, serves as a channel for spiritual light realms of All-That-Is, after his direct spiritual access was opened in 2005. Since then, almost on a daily basis, messages are being transmitted to him. In 2009 the author was asked to found the publishing house LICHTWELTVERLAG, so that the messages can find a wider distribution. Besides the many publications (printed books, ebooks), it is foremost the daily publications in the blog, which contribute to a growing number of readers.

Since the formation of the company, every month "Light Readings" take place. These are public events, where messages are being transmitted "live" to the author. This enables individuals to directly participate in the light filled reality of the heaven and watch the author personally during his work. As "GOD'S scribe" his most important task is to pass on the transmitted messages accurately, clearly and without comments.

JAHN J KASSL is a way shower, in order to accompany individuals on the way into the Light and to assist them during the transformation into the new reality of being. The author lives in Vienna, Austria, since 1983.

PUBLICATIONS BY JAHN J KASSL

Available in English as eBook:

Telos — Welcome to Agartha
Elija Prophecies 1 — 48
Elija Prophecies 49 — 65 for all 4D-Worlds until the Year 3000
The Biography of Jesus — Part I
The Biography of Jesus — Part II
Mandate for this World (for free download):
1) Put down the Weapons!
2) Reveal the Truth to the World Public
3) Act of Liberation
4) 3 Fire Rituals

The following eBooks will be published soon:

Life — Volume I
Light I — Healing by God
Light II — Healing by God
2026 — God's Revelations
Language of the Soul — 13 Keys to Life
30 Gates to Enlightenment
Class in Creation — Paul the Venetian
Class to Freedom — Babaji
Revelations Sananda — Volume I
Revelations Sananda — Volume II

All publications are available from Lichtwelt Verlag —
www.lichtweltverlag.com